MODERN SHORT STORIES

Modern Short Stories
FOR STUDENTS OF ENGLISH

selected and edited by
PETER J. W. TAYLOR

OXFORD UNIVERSITY PRESS

Oxford University Press, Walton Street, Oxford OX2 6DP

Oxford New York Toronto
Delhi Bombay Calcutta Madras Karachi
Petaling Jaya Singapore Hong Kong Tokyo
Nairobi Dar es Salaam Cape Town
Melbourne Auckland
and associated companies in
Berlin Ibadan

OXFORD, OXFORD ENGLISH and the OXFORD ENGLISH logo
are trade marks of Oxford University Press

ISBN 0 19 416707 0

© in selections and editorial matter Oxford University Press, 1968

First published 1968
Seventeenth impression 1990

Printed in Hong Kong

CONTENTS

ACKNOWLEDGEMENTS

The editor gratefully acknowledges permission from the following to reprint their material:

Elizabeth Bowen and Jonathan Cape Ltd. for 'The Demon Lover'; the trustees of the Joseph Conrad Estate and J. M. Dent and Sons Ltd. for 'The Lagoon' (*Tales of Unrest*) by Joseph Conrad; E. M. Forster and Sidgwick and Jackson Ltd. for 'The Siren' (*The Collected Short Stories of E. M. Forster*); Graham Greene and William Heinemann Ltd. for 'The End of the Party' (*Twenty-One Stories*); Laurence Pollinger Ltd. and the estate of the late Mrs. Frieda Lawrence for 'The Last Laugh' (*The Complete Short Stories of D. H. Lawrence*) by D. H. Lawrence; The Society of Authors as the literary representative of the Estate of the late Katherine Mansfield for 'Feuille D'Album' (*Bliss*) by Katharine Mansfield; the executors of W. Somerset Maugham, William Heinemann Ltd. and Doubleday and Co. Inc. for 'The Bum' (*Cosmopolitans*) by W. Somerset Maugham; The Bodley Head Ltd. for 'Sredni Vashtar' (*The Bodley Head Saki*) by Saki (H. H. Munro); A. D. Peters and Co. for 'Tactical Exercise' (*The Ordeal of Gilbert Pinfold*) by Evelyn Waugh; Leonard Woolf and The Hogarth Press for 'Kew Gardens' (*A Haunted House and Other Stories*) by Virginia Woolf.

INTRODUCTION

This volume is primarily intended for students who are preparing for the Cambridge Certificate of Proficiency in English. It should also prove valuable to many other foreign students whose English has reached a similar level and even to students in English schools.

Short stories, on account of their structure and comparative brevity, often provide a more fruitful basis for language study and discussion than any other form of fiction. They are particularly suitable for the study of English as a foreign language, and it is felt that these stories give the student an opportunity to analyse carefully the living English used by contemporary authors.

I have chosen short stories by some of the best known twentieth-century English writers in order to introduce them to the reader, and in the hope of encouraging further reading of the same authors, have included a select bibliography at the end of the volume. I have tried to use stories which cover as wide a range of themes and styles of writing as possible, and at the same time provide enjoyable and stimulating reading.

To help the student working on his own, I have given a number of notes where the meaning is not obvious from the context, or where a dictionary would either be confusing or unhelpful. The questions at the end of each story are preceded by a selection of idiomatic phrases and constructions in common usage, which should be useful to the student in his own writing and conversation. I have included the intrinsic meaning of the phrases and also referred the student to their usage within the framework of sentences in the actual text.

The questions themselves are not concerned with the purely factual content of the stories, but invite a sensitive response to the ideas and the expression of them, through the details of the language. Some direct the reader's attention to the language itself, others towards a general appreciation of the content. It is hoped that many of the questions will provide material for subsequent thought, discussion or writing about the significant ideas in the stories.

I would like to express my gratitude to my wife and also to the colleagues who have helped in compiling this volume.

P. J. W. T.

ELIZABETH BOWEN

The Demon Lover

ELIZABETH BOWEN, who was born in Dublin
in 1899, comes from an Irish family, although
she herself was educated at a school in Kent in
South-Eastern England.

She began to write short stories when she
was twenty and in 1923 her first book—a
volume of short stories under the title
Encounters—was published.

Since 1935 she has largely lived in London
and was there during the whole of the Second
World War. She has become known as a
writer of novels and short stories—often set in
London against the background of the
Second World War—and also as a literary
critic of distinction. She has received a
number of literary awards, and her two
novels *The Death of the Heart* (1938) and *The
Heat of the Day* (1949) are particularly well
known.

TOWARDS THE END of her day in London Mrs Drover went round to her shut-up house to look for several things she wanted to take away. Some belonged to herself, some to her family, who were by now used to their country life. It was late August; it had been a steamy, showery day: at the moment the trees down the pavement glittered in an escape of humid yellow afternoon sun. Against the next batch of clouds, already piling up ink-dark, broken chimneys and parapets stood out. In her once familiar street, as in any unused channel, an unfamiliar queerness had silted up; a cat wove itself in and out of railings, but no human eye watched Mrs Drover's return. Shifting some parcels under her arm, she slowly forced round her latchkey in an unwilling lock, then gave the door, which had warped, a push with her knee. Dead air came out to meet her as she went in.

The staircase window having been boarded up, no light came down into the hall. But one door, she could just see, stood ajar, so she went quickly through into the room and unshuttered the big window in there. Now the prosaic woman, looking about her, was more perplexed than she knew by everything that she saw, by traces of her long former habit of life—the yellow smoke-stain up the white marble mantelpiece, the ring left by a vase on the top of the escritoire;[1] the bruise in the wallpaper where, on the door being thrown open widely, the china handle had always hit the wall. The piano, having gone away to be stored, had left what looked like claw-marks on its part of the parquet. Though not much dust had seeped in, each object wore a film of another kind; and, the only ventilation being the chimney, the whole drawing-room smelled of the cold hearth. Mrs Drover put down her parcels on the escritoire and left the room to proceed upstairs; the things she wanted were in a bedroom chest.

She had been anxious to see how the house was—the part-time caretaker she shared with some neighbours was away this week on his holiday, known to be not yet back. At the best of times he did not look in often, and she was never sure that she trusted him. There were some cracks in the structure, left by the last bombing, on which she was anxious to keep an eye. Not that one could do anything—

A shaft of refracted daylight now lay across the hall. She stopped dead and stared at the hall table—on this lay a letter addressed to her.

She thought first—then the caretaker *must* be back. All the

[1] escritoire: a writing desk.

same, who, seeing the house shuttered, would have dropped a letter in at the box? It was not a circular,[1] it was not a bill. And the post office redirected, to the address in the country, everything for her that came through the post. The caretaker (even if he *were* back) did not know she was due in London today—her call here had been planned to be a surprise—so his negligence in the manner of this letter, leaving it to wait in the dusk and the dust, annoyed her. Annoyed, she picked up the letter, which bore no stamp. But it cannot be important, or they would know. . . . She took the letter rapidly upstairs with her, without a stop to look 10 at the writing till she reached what had been her bedroom, where she let in light. The room looked over the garden and other gardens: the sun had gone in; as the clouds sharpened and lowered, the trees and rank lawns seemed already to smoke with dark. Her reluctance to look again at the letter came from the fact that she felt intruded upon—and by someone contemptuous of her ways. However, in the tenseness preceding the fall of rain she read it: it was a few lines.

Dear Kathleen: you will not have forgotten that today is our anniversary, and the day we said. The years have gone by at once slowly 20 and fast. In view of the fact that nothing has changed, I shall rely upon you to keep your promise. I was sorry to see you leave London, but was satisfied that you would be back in time. You may expect me, therefore, at the hour arranged.

Until then . . .
K.

Mrs Drover looked for the date: it was today's. She dropped the letter on to the bed-springs, then picked it up to see the writing again—her lips, beneath the remains of lipstick, beginning to go white. She felt so much the change in her own face that she went to the mirror, polished a clear patch in it and looked at once urgently and stealthily in. She was confronted by a woman of 30 forty-four, with eyes starting out under a hat-brim that had been rather carelessly pulled down. She had not put on any more powder since she left the shop where she ate her solitary tea. The pearls her husband had given her on their marriage hung loose round her now rather thinner throat, slipping in the V of the pink wool jumper her sister knitted last autumn as they sat round the fire. Mrs Drover's most normal expression was one of controlled worry, but of assent. Since the birth of the third of

[1] circular: a printed letter sent to a number of people.

her little boys, attended by a quite serious illness, she had had an intermittent muscular flicker to the left of her mouth, but in spite of this she could always sustain a manner that was at once energetic and calm.

Turning from her own face as precipitately as she had gone to meet it, she went to the chest where the things were, unlocked it, threw up the lid and knelt to search. But as rain began to come crashing down she could not keep from looking over her shoulder at the stripped bed on which the letter lay. Behind the blanket of rain the clock of the church that still stood struck six—with rapidly heightening apprehension she counted each of the slow strokes. 'The hour arranged. . . . My God,' she said, '*what* hour? How should I . . . ? After twenty-five years. . . .'

The young girl talking to the soldier in the garden had not ever completely seen his face. It was dark; they were saying good-bye under a tree. Now and then—for it felt, from not seeing him at this intense moment, as though she had never seen him at all—she verified his presence for these few moments longer by putting out a hand, which he each time pressed, without very much kindness, and painfully, on to one of the breast buttons of his uniform. That cut of the button on the palm of her hand was, principally, what she was to carry away. This was so near the end of a leave from France that she could only wish him already gone. It was August 1916. Being not kissed, being drawn away from and looked at intimidated Kathleen till she imagined spectral glitters in the place of his eyes. Turning away and looking back up the lawn she saw, through branches of trees, the drawing-room window alight: she caught a breath for the moment when she could go running back there into the safe arms of her mother and sister, and cry: 'What shall I do, what shall I do? He has gone.'

Hearing her catch her breath, her fiancé said, without feeling: 'Cold?'

'You're going away such a long way.'

'Not so far as you think.'

'I don't understand?'

'You don't have to,' he said. 'You will. You know what we said.'

'But that was—suppose you—I mean, suppose.'

'I shall be with you,' he said, 'sooner or later. You won't forget that. You need do nothing but wait.'

4

Only a little more than a minute later she was free to run up the silent lawn. Looking in through the window at her mother and sister, who did not for the moment perceive her, she already felt that unnatural promise drive down between her and the rest of all human kind. No other way of having given herself could have made her feel so apart, lost and foresworn. She could not have plighted a more sinister troth.[1]

Kathleen behaved well when, some months later, her fiancé was reported missing, presumed killed. Her family not only supported her but were able to praise her courage without 10 stint[2] because they could not regret, as a husband for her, the man they knew almost nothing about. They hoped she would, in a year or two, console herself—and had it been only a question of consolation things might have gone much straighter ahead. But her trouble, behind just a little grief, was a complete dislocation from everything. She did not reject other lovers, for these failed to appear: for years she failed to attract men—and with the approach of her thirties she became natural enough to share her family's anxiousness on this score. She began to put herself out, to wonder; and at thirty-two she was very greatly 20 relieved to find herself being courted by William Drover. She married him, and the two of them settled down in this quiet, arboreal part of Kensington: in this house the years piled up, her children were born and they all lived till they were driven out by the bombs of the next war. Her movements as Mrs Drover were circumscribed, and she dismissed any idea that they were still watched.

As things were—dead or living the letter-writer sent her only a threat. Unable, for some minutes, to go on kneeling with her back exposed to the empty room, Mrs Drover rose from the 30 chest to sit on an upright chair whose back was firmly against the wall. The desuetude of her former bedroom, her married London home's whole air of being a cracked cup from which memory, with its reassuring power, had either evaporated or leaked away, made a crisis—and at just this crisis the letter-writer had, knowledgeably, struck. The hollowness of the house this evening cancelled years on years of voices, habits and steps. Through the shut windows she only heard rain fall on the roofs around. To rally herself, she said she was in a mood—and,

[1] to plight a troth: to make a solemn promise, usually concerning marriage.

[2] without stint: without any limits.

5

for two or three seconds shutting her eyes, told herself that she had imagined the letter. But she opened them—there it lay on the bed.

On the supernatural side of the letter's entrance she was not permitting her mind to dwell. Who, in London, knew she meant to call at the house today? Evidently, however, this had been known. The caretaker, *had* he come back, had had no cause to expect her: he would have taken the letter in his pocket, to forward it, at his own time, through the post. There was no other sign that the caretaker had been in—but, if not? Letters 10 dropped in at doors of deserted houses do not fly or walk to tables in halls. They do not sit on the dust of empty tables with the air of certainty that they will be found. There is needed some human hand—but nobody but the caretaker had a key. Under circumstances she did not care to consider, a house can be entered without a key. It was possible that she was not alone now. She might be being waited for, downstairs. Waited for—until when? Until 'the hour arranged'. At least that was not six o'clock: six had struck.

She rose from the chair and went over and locked the door. 20

The thing was, to get out. To fly? No, not that: she had to catch her train. As a woman whose utter dependability was the keystone of her family life she was not willing to return to the country, to her husband, her little boys and her sister, without the objects she had come up to fetch. Resuming work at the chest she set about making up a number of parcels in a rapid, fumbling-decisive way. These, with her shopping parcels, would be too much to carry; these meant a taxi—at the thought of the taxi her heart went up and her normal breathing resumed. I will ring up the taxi now; the taxi cannot come too 30 soon: I shall hear the taxi out there running its engine, till I walk calmly down to it through the hall. I'll ring up—But no: the telephone is cut off.[1] . . . She tugged at a knot she had tied wrong.

The idea of flight. . . . He was never kind to me, not really. I don't remember him kind at all. Mother said he never considered me. He was set on me, that was what it was—not love. Not love, not meaning a person well. What did he do, to make me promise like that? I can't remember—But she found that she could.   40

She remembered with such dreadful acuteness that the

[1] cut off: disconnected.

twenty-five years since then dissolved like smoke and she instinctively looked for the weal left by the button on the palm of her hand. She remembered not only all that he said and did but the complete suspension of *her* existence during that August week. I was not myself—they all told me so at the time. She remembered—but with one white burning blank as where acid has dropped on a photograph: *under no conditions* could she remember his face.

So, wherever he may be waiting, I shall not know him. You have no time to run from a face you do not expect.   10

The thing was to get to the taxi before any clock struck what could be the hour. She would slip[1] down the street and round the side of the square to where the square gave on the main road. She would return in the taxi, safe, to her own door, and bring the solid driver into the house with her to pick up the parcels from room to room. The idea of the taxi driver made her decisive, bold: she unlocked her door, went to the top of the staircase and listened down.

She heard nothing—but while she was hearing nothing the *passé* air[2] of the staircase was disturbed by a draught that 20 travelled up to her face. It emanated from the basement: down there a door or window was being opened by someone who chose this moment to leave the house.

The rain had stopped; the pavements steamily shone as Mrs Drover let herself out by inches from her own front door into the empty street. The unoccupied houses opposite continued to meet her look with their damaged stare. Making towards the thoroughfare and the taxi, she tried not to keep looking behind. Indeed, the silence was so intense—one of those creeks of London silence exaggerated this summer by the damage of war—that no tread 30 could have gained on hers unheard. Where her street debouched on the square where people went on living, she grew conscious of, and checked, her unnatural pace. Across the open end of the square two buses impassively passed each other: women, a perambulator, cyclists, a man wheeling a barrow signalized, once again, the ordinary flow of life. At the square's most populous corner should be—and was—the short taxi rank. This evening, only one taxi—but this, although it presented its black rump, appeared already to be alertly waiting for her. Indeed, without looking round the driver started his engine as 40

[1] slip: to move quickly.
[2] *passé* air: stale air which has not circulated for some time.

7

she panted up from behind and put her hand on the door. As she did so, the clock struck seven. The taxi faced the main road: to make the trip back to her house it would *have* to turn—she had settled back on the seat and the taxi *had* turned before she, surprised by its knowing movement, recollected that she had not 'said where'. She leaned forward to scratch at the glass panel that divided the driver's head from her own.

The driver braked to what was almost a stop, turned round and slid the glass panel back: the jolt of this flung Mrs Drover forward till her face was almost into the glass. Through the aperture driver and passenger, not six inches between them, remained for an eternity eye to eye. Mrs Drover's mouth hung open for some seconds before she could issue her first scream. After that she continued to scream freely and to beat with her gloved hands on the glass all round as the taxi, accelerating without mercy, made off with her into the hinterland of deserted streets.

Useful Phrases

1 to look in (page 2, line 34)—to visit briefly.
2 to keep an eye on (page 2, line 36)—to watch carefully or look after.
3 to stop dead (page 2, line 39)—to stop very suddenly through shock or surprise.
4 on this score (page 5, line 19)—concerning this particular matter.
5 to put oneself out (page 5, lines 19 & 20)—to upset oneself (sometimes also to bother to do something troublesome for others).
6 to be set on someone (page 6, line 37)—to be determined to have someone as a wife, etc.

Questions to guide the reader and also for further discussion or essay writing

1 Explain carefully what the writer is trying to express in the following quotations:
a 'trees down the pavement glittered in an escape of humid yellow afternoon sun' (page 2, lines 5 & 6).
b 'the prosaic woman' (page 2, line 18).
c 'the trees and rank lawns seemed already to smoke with dark' (page 3, lines 14 & 15).

8

d 'the solid driver' (page 7, line 15).

e 'The unoccupied houses opposite continued to meet her look with their damaged stare' (page 7, lines 26 & 27).

f 'one of those creeks of London silence exaggerated this summer by the damage of war—' (page 7, lines 29 & 30).

2 Why was Mrs. Drover somewhat reluctant to return to her house in London?

3 What sort of woman does the story suggest Mrs. Drover is?

4 What interpretation do you place upon the ending of the story?

JOSEPH CONRAD

The Lagoon

JOSEPH CONRAD, the son of a Polish writer, was born in Poland in 1857. He was brought up by an uncle, and educated himself by reading widely in both Polish and French. In 1874 he went to Marseille to become a sailor, and later joined an English cargo ship on which he first visited England in 1878.

He travelled extensively as a British sailor, and eventually reached the rank of Captain. In 1886 he became a naturalized British subject, and in the same year began his first book—*Almayer's Folly*—which was published in 1895.

The success of this book, together with his increasing ill-health, made him decide to give up the sea and turn to writing instead. In 1896 he married and settled near London.

Before his death in 1924 he had won wide popularity and acclaim as a novelist. He used his experience and knowledge of the sea as a background for many of his novels, and at his best, he is one of the greatest of modern English prose writers.

THE WHITE MAN, leaning with both arms over the roof of the little house in the stern of the boat, said to the steersman:

'We will pass the night in Arsat's clearing. It is late.'

The Malay only grunted, and went on looking fixedly at the river. The white man rested his chin on his crossed arms and gazed at the wake[1] of the boat. At the end of the straight avenue of forests cut by the intense glitter of the river, the sun appeared unclouded and dazzling, poised low over the water that shone smoothly like a band of metal. The forests, sombre and dull, stood motionless and silent on each side of the broad stream. At the foot of big, towering trees, trunkless nipa palms rose from the mud of the bank, in bunches of leaves enormous and heavy, that hung unstirring over the brown swirl of eddies. In the still-ness of the air every tree, every leaf, every bough, every tendril of creeper and every petal of minute blossoms seemed to have been bewitched into an immobility perfect and final. Nothing moved on the river but the eight paddles that rose flashing regularly, dipped together with a single splash; while the steersman swept right and left with a periodic and sudden flourish of his blade describing a glinting semicircle above his head. The churned-up water frothed alongside with a confused murmur. And the white man's canoe, advancing upstream in the short-lived disturbance of its own making, seemed to enter the portals of a land from which the very memory of motion had for ever departed.

The white man, turning his back upon the setting sun, looked along the empty and broad expanse of the sea-reach. For the last three miles of its course the wandering, hesitating river, as if enticed irresistibly by the freedom of an open horizon, flows straight into the sea, flows straight to the east—to the east that harbours both light and darkness. Astern of the boat the re-peated call of some bird, a cry discordant and feeble, skipped along over the smooth water and lost itself, before it could reach the other shore, in the breathless silence of the world.

The steersman dug his paddle into the stream, and held hard with stiffened arms, his body thrown forward. The water gurgled aloud; and suddenly the long straight reach seemed to pivot on its centre, the forests swung in a semicircle, and the slanting beams of sunset touched the broadside of the canoe with a fiery glow, throwing the slender and distorted shadows of its crew upon the streaked glitter of the river. The white man

[1] the wake: the disturbed water left behind a boat as it moves along.

11

turned to look ahead. The course of the boat had been altered at right-angles to the stream, and the carved dragon-head of its prow was pointing now at a gap in the fringing bushes of the bank. It glided through, brushing the overhanging twigs, and disappeared from the river like some slim and amphibious creature leaving the water for its lair in the forests.

The narrow creek was like a ditch: tortuous, fabulously deep; filled with gloom under the thin strip of pure and shining blue of the heaven. Immense trees soared up, invisible behind the festooned draperies of creepers. Here and there, near the glisten- 10 ing blackness of the water, a twisted root of some tall tree showed amongst the tracery of small ferns, black and dull, writhing and motionless, like an arrested snake. The short words of the paddlers reverberated loudly between the thick and sombre walls of vegetation. Darkness oozed out from be- tween the trees, through the tangled maze of the creepers, from behind the great fantastic and unstirring leaves; the darkness, mysterious and invincible; the darkness scented and poisonous of impenetrable forests.

The men poled in the shoaling water.[1] The creek broadened, 20 opening out into a wide sweep of a stagnant lagoon. The forests receded from the marshy bank, leaving a level strip of bright green, reedy grass to frame the reflected blueness of the sky. A fleecy pink cloud drifted high above, trailing the delicate colour- ing of its image under the floating leaves and the silvery blossoms of the lotus. A little house, perched on high piles, appeared black in the distance. Near it, two tall nibong palms, that seemed to have come out of the forests in the background, leaned slightly over the ragged roof, with a suggestion of sad tenderness and care in the droop of their leafy and soaring heads. 30

The steersman, pointing with his paddle, said, 'Arsat is there. I see his canoe fast[2] between the piles.'

The polers ran along the sides of the boat glancing over their shoulders at the end of the day's journey. They would have preferred to spend the night somewhere else than on this lagoon of weird aspect and ghostly reputation. Moreover, they disliked Arsat, first as a stranger, and also because he who repairs a ruined house, and dwells in it, proclaims that he is not afraid to live amongst the spirits that haunt the places abandoned by mankind. Such a man can disturb the course of fate by glances 40

[1] shoaling water: water which is becoming shallow.

[2] fast: here means, securely tied up, moored.

or words; while his familiar ghosts are not easy to propitiate by casual wayfarers upon whom they long to wreak the malice of their human master. White men care not for such things, being unbelievers and in league with the Father of Evil, who leads them unharmed through the invisible dangers of this world. To the warnings of the righteous they oppose an offensive pretence of disbelief. What is there to be done?

So they thought, throwing their weight on the end of their long poles. The big canoe glided on swiftly, noiselessly, and smoothly, towards Arsat's clearing, till, in a great rattling of poles thrown down, and the loud murmurs of 'Allah be praised!' it came with a gentle knock against the crooked piles below the house.

The boatmen with uplifted faces shouted discordantly, 'Arsat! O Arsat!' Nobody came. The white man began to climb the rude ladder giving access to the bamboo platform before the house. The juragan[1] of the boat said sulkily, 'We will cook in the sampan,[2] and sleep on the water.'

'Pass my blankets and the basket,' said the white man, curtly.

He knelt on the edge of the platform to receive the bundle. Then the boat shoved off, and the white man, standing up, confronted Arsat, who had come out through the low door of his hut. He was a man young, powerful, with a broad chest and muscular arms. He had nothing on but his sarong.[3] His head was bare. His big, soft eyes stared eagerly at the white man, but his voice and demeanour were composed as he asked, without any words of greeting:

'Have you medicine, Tuan?'

'No,' said the visitor in a startled tone. 'No. Why? Is there sickness in the house?'

'Enter and see,' replied Arsat, in the same calm manner, and turning short round, passed again through the small doorway. The white man, dropping his bundles, followed.

In the dim light of the dwelling he made out on a couch of bamboos a woman stretched on her back under a broad sheet of red cotton cloth. She lay still, as if dead; but her big eyes, wide open, glittered in the gloom, staring upwards at the slender

[1] juragan: the chief man on the boat.
[2] sampan: a type of Eastern boat.
[3] sarong: a form of clothing worn in the East; a cloth wrapped round the lower part of the body.

JOSEPH CONRAD

rafters, motionless and unseeing. She was in a high fever, and
evidently unconscious. Her cheeks were sunk slightly, her lips
were partly open, and on the young face there was the ominous
and fixed expression—the absorbed, contemplating expression
of the unconscious who are going to die. The two men stood
looking down at her in silence.

'Has she been long ill?' asked the traveller.

'I have not slept for five nights,' answered the Malay, in a
deliberate tone. 'At first she heard voices calling her from the
water and struggled against me who held her. But since the sun
of to-day rose she hears nothing—she hears not me. She sees
nothing. She sees not me—me!'

He remained silent for a minute, then asked softly:

'Tuan, will she die?'

'I fear so,' said the white man, sorrowfully. He had known
Arsat years ago, in a far country in times of trouble and danger,
when no friendship is to be despised. And since his Malay friend
had come unexpectedly to dwell in the hut on the lagoon with
a strange woman, he had slept many times there, in his journeys
up and down the river. He liked the man who knew how to keep
faith in council and how to fight without fear by the side of his
white friend. He liked him—not so much perhaps as a man likes
his favourite dog—but still he liked him well enough to help
and ask no questions, to think sometimes vaguely and hazily in
the midst of his own pursuits, about the lonely man and the long-
haired woman with audacious face and triumphant eyes, who
lived together hidden by the forests—alone and feared.

The white man came out of the hut in time to see the enormous
conflagration of sunset put out by the swift and stealthy shadows
that, rising like a black and impalpable vapour above the tree-
tops, spread over the heaven, extinguishing the crimson glow of
floating clouds and the red brilliance of departing daylight. In a
few moments all the stars came out above the intense blackness
of the earth and the great lagoon gleaming suddenly with reflected lights resembled an oval patch of night sky flung down
into the hopeless and abysmal night of the wilderness. The white
man had some supper out of the basket, then collecting a few
sticks that lay about the platform, made up a small fire, not for
warmth, but for the sake of the smoke, which would keep off the
mosquitos. He wrapped himself in the blankets and sat with his
back against the reed wall of the house, smoking thoughtfully.

Arsat came through the doorway with noiseless steps and

14

squatted down by the fire. The white man moved his out-stretched legs a little.

'She breathes,' said Arsat in a low voice, anticipating the expected question. 'She breathes and burns as if with a great fire. She speaks not; she hears not—and burns!'

He paused for a moment, then asked in a quiet, incurious tone:

'Tuan . . . will she die?'

The white man moved his shoulders uneasily, and muttered in a hesitating manner:

'If such is her fate.'

'No, Tuan,' said Arsat, calmly. 'If such is my fate. I hear, I see, I wait, I remember . . . Tuan, do you remember the old days? Do you remember my brother?'

'Yes,' said the white man. The Malay rose suddenly and went in. The other, sitting still outside, could hear the voice in the hut. Arsat said: 'Hear me! Speak!' His words were succeeded by a complete silence. 'O Diamelen!'[1] he cried, suddenly. After that cry there was a deep sigh. Arsat came out and sank down again in his old place.

They sat in silence before the fire. There was no sound within the house, there was no sound near them; but far away on the lagoon they could hear the voices of the boatmen ringing fitful[2] and distinct on the calm water. The fire in the bows of the sampan shone faintly in the distance with a hazy red glow. Then it died out. The voices ceased. The land and the water slept invisible, unstirring and mute. It was as though there had been nothing left in the world but the glitter of stars streaming, ceaseless and vain, through the black stillness of the night.

The white man gazed straight before him into the darkness with wide-open eyes. The fear and fascination, the inspiration and the wonder of death—of death near, unavoidable, and un-seen, soothed the unrest of his race and stirred the most in-distinct, the most intimate of his thoughts. The ever-ready suspicion of evil, the gnawing suspicion that lurks in our hearts, flowed out into the stillness round him—into the stillness pro-found and dumb, and made it appear untrustworthy and infamous, like the placid and impenetrable mask of an unjusti-fiable violence. In that fleeting and powerful disturbance of his being the earth enfolded in the starlight peace became a shadowy

[1] Diamelen: the name of the woman Arsat lives with.
[2] fitful: from time to time.

country of inhuman strife, a battle-field of phantoms terrible and
charming, august or ignoble, struggling ardently for the possession of our helpless hearts. An unquiet and mysterious country of
inextinguishable desires and fears.

A plaintive murmur rose in the night; a murmur saddening
and startling, as if the great solitudes of surrounding woods had
tried to whisper into his ear the wisdom of their immense and
lofty indifference. Sounds hesitating and vague floated in the air
round him, shaped themselves slowly into words; and at last
flowed on gently in a murmuring stream of soft and mono- 10
tonous sentences. He stirred like a man waking up and changed
his position slightly. Arsat, motionless and shadowy, sitting with
bowed head under the stars, was speaking in a low and dreamy
tone:

'. . . for where can we lay down the heaviness of our trouble
but in a friend's heart? A man must speak of war and of love.
You, Tuan, know what war is, and you have seen me in time of
danger seek death as other men seek life! A writing may be lost;
a lie may be written; but what the eye has seen is truth and
remains in the mind!' 20

'I remember,' said the white man, quietly. Arsat went on with
mournful composure:

'Therefore I shall speak to you of love. Speak in the night.
Speak before both night and love are gone—and the eye of day
looks upon my sorrow and my shame; upon my blackened face;
upon my burnt-up heart.'

A sigh, short and faint, marked an almost imperceptible
pause, and then his words flowed on, without a stir, without a
gesture.

'After the time of trouble and war was over and you went 30
away from my country in the pursuit of your desires, which we,
men of the islands, cannot understand, I and my brother
became again, as we had been before, the sword-bearers of the
Ruler. You know we were men of family, belonging to a ruling
race, and more fit than any to carry on our right shoulder the
emblem of power. And in the time of prosperity Si Dendring
showed us favour, as we, in time of sorrow, had showed to him
the faithfulness of our courage. It was a time of peace. A time of
deer-hunts and cock-fights; of idle talks and foolish squabbles
between men whose bellies are full and weapons are rusty. But 40
the sower watched the young rice-shoots grow up without fear,
and the traders came and went, departed lean and returned fat

into the river of peace. They brought news, too. Brought lies and truth mixed together, so that no man knew when to rejoice and when to be sorry. We heard from them about you also. They had seen you here and had seen you there. And I was glad to hear, for I remembered the stirring times, and I always remembered you, Tuan, till the time came when my eyes could see nothing in the past, because they had looked upon the one who is dying there—in the house.'

He stopped to exclaim in an intense whisper, 'O Mara bahia![1] O Calamity!' then went on speaking a little louder: 10

'There's no worse enemy and no better friend than a brother, Tuan, for one brother knows another, and in perfect knowledge is strength for good or evil. I loved my brother. I went to him and told him that I could see nothing but one face, hear nothing but one voice. He told me: "Open your heart so that she can see what is in it—and wait. Patience is wisdom. Inchi Midah may die or our Ruler may throw off his fear of a woman!". . . . I waited!. . . . You remember the lady with the veiled face, Tuan, and the fear of our Ruler before her cunning and temper. And if she wanted her servant, what could I do? But I fed the hunger 20 of my heart on short glances and stealthy words. I loitered on the path to the bath-houses in the daytime, and when the sun had fallen behind the forest I crept along the jasmine hedges of the women's courtyard. Unseeing, we spoke to one another through the scent of flowers, through the veil of leaves, through the blades of long grass that stood still before our lips; so great was our prudence, so faint was the murmur of our great longing. The time passed swiftly . . . and there were whispers amongst women—and our enemies watched—my brother was gloomy, and I began to think of killing and of a fierce death. . . . We are 30 of a people who take what they want—like you whites. There is a time when a man should forget loyalty and respect. Might and authority are given to rulers, but to all men is given love and strength and courage. My brother said, "You shall take her from their midst. We are two who are like one." And I answered, "Let it be soon, for I find no warmth in sunlight that does not shine upon her." Our time came when the Ruler and all the great people went to the mouth of the river to fish by torchlight. There were hundreds of boats, and on the white sand, between the water and the forests, dwellings of leaves were built for the 40 households of the Rajahs.[2] The smoke of cooking-fires was like a

[1] Mara bahia: danger.   [2] Rajahs: princes or chiefs.

blue mist of the evening, and many voices rang in it joyfully. While they were making the boats ready to beat up the fish, my brother came to me and said, "To-night!" I looked to my weapons, and when the time came our canoe took its place in the circle of boats carrying the torches. The lights blazed on the water, but behind the boats there was darkness. When the shouting began and the excitement made them like mad we dropped out. The water swallowed our fire, and we floated back to the shore that was dark with only here and there the glimmer of embers. We could hear the talk of slave-girls amongst the 10 sheds. Then we found a place deserted and silent. We waited there. She came. She came running along the shore, rapid and leaving no trace, like a leaf driven by the wind into the sea. My brother said gloomily, "Go and take her; carry her into our boat." I lifted her in my arms. She panted. Her heart was beating against my breast. I said, "I take you from those people. You came to the cry of my heart, but my arms take you into my boat against the will of the great!" "It is right," said my brother. "We are men who take what we want and can hold it against many. We should have taken her in daylight." I said, "Let us be 20 off"; for since she was in my boat I began to think of our Ruler's many men. "Yes. Let us be off," said my brother. "We are cast out and this boat is our country now—and the sea is our refuge." He lingered with his foot on the shore, and I entreated him to hasten, for I remembered the strokes of her heart against my breast and thought that two men cannot withstand a hundred. We left, paddling down-stream close to the bank; and as we passed by the creek where they were fishing, the great shouting had ceased, but the murmur of voices was loud like the humming of insects flying at noonday. The boats floated, clustered to- 30 gether, in the red light of torches, under a black roof of smoke; and men talked of their sport. Men that boasted, and praised, and jeered—men that would have been our friends in the morning, but on that night were already our enemies. We paddled swiftly past. We had no more friends in the country of our birth. She sat in the middle of the canoe with covered face; silent as she is now; unseeing as she is now—and I had no regret at what I was leaving because I could hear her breathing close to me—as I can hear her now.'

He paused, listened with his ear turned to the doorway, then 40 shook his head and went on:

'My brother wanted to shout the cry of challenge—one cry

only—to let the people know we were freeborn robbers who trusted our arms and the great sea. And again I begged him in the name of our love to be silent. Could I not hear her breathing close to me? I knew the pursuit would come quick enough. My brother loved me. He dipped his paddle without a splash. He only said, "There is half a man in you now—the other half is in that woman. I can wait. When you are a whole man again, you will come back with me here to shout defiance. We are sons of the same mother." I made no answer. All my strength and all my spirit were in my hands that held the paddle—for I longed to 10 be with her in a safe place beyond the reach of men's anger and of women's spite. My love was so great, that I thought it could guide me to a country where death was unknown, if I could only escape from Inchi Midah's fury and from our Ruler's sword. We paddled with haste, breathing through our teeth. The blades bit deep into the smooth water. We passed out of the river; we flew in clear channels amongst the shallows. We skirted the black coast; we skirted the sand beaches where the sea speaks in whispers to the land; and the gleam of white sand flashed back past our boat, so swiftly she ran upon the water. We spoke not. 20 Only once I said, "Sleep, Diamelen, for soon you may want all your strength." I heard the sweetness of her voice, but I never turned my head. The sun rose and still we went on. Water fell from my face like rain from a cloud. We flew in the light and heat. I never looked back, but I knew that my brother's eyes, behind me, were looking steadily ahead, for the boat went as straight as a bushman's dart, when it leaves the end of the sumpitan.[1] There was no better paddler, no better steersman than my brother. Many times, together, we had won races in that canoe. But we never had put out our strength as we did then— 30 then, when for the last time we paddled together! There was no braver or stronger man in our country than my brother. I could not spare the strength to turn my head and look at him, but every moment I heard the hiss of his breath getting louder behind me. Still he did not speak. The sun was high. The heat clung to my back like a flame of fire. My ribs were ready to burst, but I could no longer get enough air into my chest. And then I felt I must cry out with my last breath, "Let us rest!" . . . "Good!" he answered; and his voice was firm. He was strong. He was brave. He knew not fear and no fatigue. . . . My brother!' 40

A murmur powerful and gentle, a murmur vast and faint; the

[1] sumpitan: a Malayan blow-gun used for shooting poisoned arrows.

19

murmur of trembling leaves, of stirring boughs, ran through the tangled depths of the forests, ran over the starry smoothness of the lagoon, and the water between the piles lapped the slimy timber once with a sudden splash. A breath of warm air touched the two men's faces and passed on with a mournful sound—a breath loud and short like an uneasy sigh of the dreaming earth.

Arsat went on in an even, low voice.

'We ran our canoe on the white beach of a little bay close to a long tongue of land that seemed to bar our road; a long wooded cape going far into the sea. My brother knew that place. 10 Beyond the cape a river has its entrance, and through the jungle of that land there is a narrow path. We made a fire and cooked rice. Then we lay down to sleep on the soft sand in the shade of our canoe, while she watched. No sooner had I closed my eyes than I heard her cry of alarm. We leaped up. The sun was half-way down the sky already, and coming in sight in the opening of the bay we saw a prau[1] manned by many paddlers. We knew it at once; it was one of our Rajah's praus. They were watching the shore, and saw us. They beat the gong, and turned the head of the prau into the bay. I felt my heart become weak within 20 my breast. Diamelen sat on the sand and covered her face. There was no escape by sea. My brother laughed. He had the gun you had given him, Tuan, before you went away, but there was only a handful of powder. He spoke to me quickly: "Run with her along the path. I shall keep them back, for they have no firearms, and landing in the face of a man with a gun is certain death for some. Run with her. On the other side of that wood there is a fisherman's house—and a canoe. When I have fired all the shots I will follow. I am a great runner, and before they can come up we shall be gone. I will hold out as long as I 30 can, for she is but a woman—that can neither run nor fight, but she has your heart in her weak hands." He dropped behind the canoe. The prau was coming. She and I ran, and as we rushed along the path I heard shots. My brother fired—once—twice— and the booming of the gong ceased. There was silence behind us. That neck of land is narrow. Before I heard my brother fire the third shot I saw the shelving[2] shore, and I saw the water again: the mouth of a broad river. We crossed a grassy glade. We ran down to the water. I saw a low hut above the black mud, and a small canoe hauled up. I heard another shot behind me. I 40

[1] prau: a long Malayan boat propelled by sails or oars.
[2] shelving: sloping down.

thought, "That is his last charge." We rushed down to the canoe; a man came running from the hut, but I leaped on him, and we rolled together in the mud. Then I got up, and he lay still at my feet. I don't know whether I had killed him or not. I and Diamelen pushed the canoe afloat. I heard yells behind me, and I saw my brother run across the glade. Many men were bounding after him; I took her in my arms and threw her into the boat, then leaped in myself. When I looked back I saw that my brother had fallen. He fell and was up again, but the men were closing round him. He shouted, "I am coming!" The men were close to him. I looked. Many men. Then I looked at her. Tuan, I pushed the canoe! I pushed it into deep water. She was kneeling forward looking at me, and I said, "Take your paddle," while I struck the water with mine. Tuan, I heard him cry. I heard him cry my name twice; and I heard voices shouting, "Kill! Strike!" I never turned back. I heard him calling my name again with a great shriek, as when life is going out together with the voice—and I never turned my head. My own name! . . . My brother! Three times he called—but I was not afraid of life. Was she not there in that canoe? And could I not with her find a country where death is forgotten—where death is unknown!'

The white man sat up. Arsat rose and stood, an indistinct and silent figure above the dying embers of the fire. Over the lagoon a mist drifting and low had crept, erasing slowly the glittering images of the stars. And now a great expanse of white vapour covered the land: it flowed cold and grey in the darkness, eddied in noiseless whirls round the tree-trunks and about the platform of the house, which seemed to float upon a restless and impalpable illusion of a sea. Only far away the tops of the trees stood outlined on the twinkle of heaven, like a sombre and forbidding shore—a coast deceptive, pitiless and black.

Arsat's voice vibrated loudly in the profound peace.

'I had her there! I had her! To get her I would have faced all mankind. But I had her—and—'

His words went out ringing into the empty distances. He paused, and seemed to listen to them dying away very far—beyond help and beyond recall. Then he said quietly:

'Tuan, I loved my brother.'

A breath of wind made him shiver. High above his head, high above the silent sea of mist, the drooping leaves of the palms rattled together with a mournful and expiring sound.

The white man stretched his legs. His chin rested on his chest, and he murmured sadly without lifting his head:

'We all love our brothers.'

Arsat burst out with an intense whispering violence:

'What did I care who died? I wanted peace in my own heart.'

He seemed to hear a stir in the house—listened—then stepped in noiselessly. The white man stood up. A breeze was coming in fitful puffs. The stars shone paler as if they had retreated into the frozen depths of immense space. After a chill gust of wind there were a few seconds of perfect calm and absolute silence. Then from behind the black and wavy line of the forests a column of golden light shot up into the heavens and spread over the semi-circle of the eastern horizon. The sun had risen. The mist lifted, broke into drifting patches, vanished into thin flying wreaths; and the unveiled lagoon lay, polished and black, in the heavy shadows at the foot of the wall of trees. A white eagle rose over it with a slanting and ponderous flight, reached the clear sunshine and appeared dazzlingly brilliant for a moment, then soaring higher, became a dark and motionless speck before it vanished into the blue as if it had left the earth for ever. The white man, standing gazing upwards before the doorway, heard in the hut a confused and broken murmur of distracted words ending with a loud groan. Suddenly Arsat stumbled out with outstretched hands, shivered, and stood still for some time with fixed eyes. Then he said:

'She burns no more.'

Before his face the sun showed its edge above the tree-tops, rising steadily. The breeze freshened; a great brilliance burst upon the lagoon, sparkled on the rippling water. The forests came out of the clear shadows of the morning, became distinct, as if they had rushed nearer—to stop short in a great stir of leaves, of nodding boughs, of swaying branches. In the merciless sunshine the whisper of unconscious life grew louder, speaking in an incomprehensible voice round the dumb darkness of that human sorrow. Arsat's eyes wandered slowly, then stared at the rising sun.

'I can see nothing,' he said half aloud to himself.

'There is nothing,' said the white man, moving to the edge of the platform and waving his hand to his boat. A shout came faintly over the lagoon and the sampan began to glide towards the abode of the friend of ghosts.

'If you want to come with me, I will wait all the morning,' said the white man, looking away upon the water.

'No, Tuan,' said Arsat, softly. 'I shall not eat or sleep in this house, but I must first see my road. Now I can see nothing—see nothing! There is no light and no peace in the world; but there is death—death for many. We were sons of the same mother—and I left him in the midst of enemies; but I am going back now.'

He drew a long breath and went on in a dreamy tone: 'In a little while I shall see clear enough to strike—to strike. But she has died, and . . . now . . . darkness.'   10

He flung his arms wide open, let them fall along his body, then stood still with unmoved face and stony eyes, staring at the sun. The white man got down into his canoe. The polers ran smartly along the sides of the boat, looking over their shoulders at the beginning of a weary journey. High in the stern, his head muffled up in white rags, the juragan sat moody, letting his paddle trail in the water. The white man, leaning with both arms over the grass roof of the little cabin, looked back at the shining ripple of the boat's wake. Before the sampan passed out of the lagoon into the creek he lifted his eyes. Arsat had not   20 moved. He stood lonely in the searching sunshine; and he looked beyond the great light of a cloudless day into the darkness of a world of illusions.

Useful Phrases

1 in league with (page 13, line 4)—allied to, joined by some bond.
2 to make out (page 13, line 35)—to identify or discern.
3 to be off (page 18, line 20)—to go, depart.
4 a handful of (page 20, line 24)—a small amount.
5 to hold out (page 20, line 30)—to remain in a place irrespective of danger or adverse conditions.
6 to stop short (page 22, line 32)—to stop suddenly or abruptly.

Questions to guide the reader and also for further discussion or essay writing

1 Explain carefully what the author is trying to express in the following quotations:
a 'the breathless silence of the world' (page 11, line 34).
b 'Darkness oozed out from between the trees' (page 12, lines 15 & 16).

B   23

c 'The blades bit deep into the smooth water' (page 19, lines 15 & 16).

d 'We skirted the black coast;' (page 19, lines 17 & 18).

e 'nodding boughs,' (page 22, line 33).

f 'the searching sunshine;' (page 23, line 21).

2 What are the respective roles of Arsat and the white man in the story?

3 Contrast Arsat with his brother from what you learn about them.

4 Is the main theme of the story one of death, guilt, or love?

5 'A writing may be lost; a lie may be written; but what the eye has seen is truth and remains in the mind!' (Page 16, lines 18–20). What does Conrad mean by this? Enlarge upon this idea.

6 'There's no worse enemy and no better friend than a brother, Tuan, for one brother knows another, and in perfect knowledge is strength for good or evil' (page 17, lines 11–13). How far do you agree with this?

7 'There is a time when a man should forget loyalty and respect' (page 17, lines 31 & 32). Would you defend Arsat's action in the story? To what extent do you agree with his statement?

E. M. FORSTER

The Story of the Siren*

E. M. FORSTER was born in London in 1879
and was educated at Tonbridge and King's
College, Cambridge. His first novel *Where
Angels Fear to Tread* was published in 1905
when he was twenty-six. He travelled
extensively, and in 1910 made his first visit to
India, the country which was to be the
setting for his last and greatest novel—*A
Passage to India* (1924).

Although he has written comparatively few
novels he has established a very high
reputation as a novelist, and has supported this
with a number of well-known short stories and
works of non-fiction.

Forster lived for many years in
Cambridge, where he was an honorary fellow of
King's College. He died in 1970.

* the Siren: a legendary sea nymph whose song charmed sailors and led
them to destruction.

FEW THINGS HAVE been more beautiful than my notebook on the Deist Controversy[1] as it fell downward through the waters of the Mediterranean. It dived, like a piece of black slate, but opened soon, disclosing leaves of pale green, which quivered into blue. Now it had vanished, now it was a piece of magical india-rubber stretching out to infinity, now it was a book again, but bigger than the book of all knowledge. It grew more fantastic as it reached the bottom, where a puff of sand welcomed it and obscured it from view. But it reappeared, quite sane though a little tremulous, lying decently open on its back, while unseen fingers fidgeted among its leaves.

'It is such a pity,' said my aunt, 'that you will not finish your work in the hotel. Then you would be free to enjoy yourself and this would never have happened.'

'Nothing of it but will change into something rich and strange,' warbled the chaplain, while his sister said, 'Why, it's gone in the water!' As for the boatmen, one of them laughed, while the other, without a word of warning, stood up and began to take his clothes off.

'Holy Moses![2] cried the Colonel. 'Is the fellow mad?'

'Yes, thank him, dear,' said my aunt: 'that is to say, tell him he is very kind, but perhaps another time.'

'All the same I do want my book back,' I complained. 'It's for my Fellowship Dissertation.[3] There won't be much left of it by another time.'

'I have an idea,' said some woman or other through her parasol. 'Let us leave this child of nature to dive for the book while we go on to the other grotto. We can land him either on this rock or on the ledge inside, and he will be ready when we return.'

The idea seemed good; and I improved it by saying I would be left behind too, to lighten the boat. So the two of us were deposited outside the little grotto on a great sunlit rock that guarded the harmonies within. Let us call them blue, though they suggest rather the spirit of what is clean—cleanliness passed from the domestic to the sublime, the cleanliness of all the sea gathered together and radiating light. The Blue Grotto at Capri[4]

---

[1] Deist Controversy: a dispute about the belief in the existence of God.

[2] Holy Moses: an exclamation of surprise or horror.

[3] Fellowship Dissertation: a piece of research undertaken in connexion with a post in a university.

[4] Capri: a small island off the South West coast of Italy.

contains only more blue water, not bluer water. That colour and that spirit is the heritage of every cave in the Mediterranean into which the sun can shine and the sea flow.

As soon as the boat left I realised how imprudent I had been to trust myself on a sloping rock with an unknown Sicilian.[1] With a jerk he became alive, seizing my arm and saying: 'Go to the end of the grotto, and I will show you something beautiful.'

He made me jump off the rock on to the ledge over a dazzling crack of sea; he drew me away from the light till I was standing on the tiny beach of sand which emerged like powdered tur- 10 quoise at the farther end. There he left me with his clothes, and returned swiftly to the summit of the entrance rock. For a moment he stood naked in the brilliant sun, looking down at the spot where the book lay. Then he crossed himself,[2] raised his hands above his head, and dived.

If the book was wonderful, the man is past all description. His effect was that of a silver statue, alive beneath the sea, through whom life throbbed in blue and green. Something infinitely happy, infinitely wise—but it was impossible that it should emerge from the depths sunburned and dripping, holding 20 the notebook on the Deist Controversy between its teeth.

A gratuity is generally expected by those who bathe. Whatever I offered, he was sure to want more, and I was disinclined for an argument in a place so beautiful and also so solitary. It was a relief that he should say in conversational tones, 'In a place like this one might see the Siren.'

I was delighted with him for thus falling into the key of his surroundings. We had been left together in a magic world, apart from all the commonplaces that are called reality, a world of blue whose floor was the sea and whose walls and roof of rock 30 trembled with the sea's reflections. Here only the fantastic would be tolerable, and it was in that spirit I echoed his words, 'One might easily see the Siren.'

He watched me curiously while he dressed. I was parting the sticky leaves of the notebook as I sat on the sand.

'Ah,' he said at last. 'You may have read the little book that was printed last year. Who would have thought that our Siren would have given the foreigners pleasure!'

[1] Sicilian: a person from Sicily, an island which lies at the foot of Italy.

[2] crossed himself: a ritual gesture of touching the forehead, breast and shoulder in the sign of the cross.

27

(I read it afterwards. Its account is, not unnaturally, incomplete, in spite of there being a woodcut[1] of the young person, and the words of her song.)

'She comes out of this blue water, doesn't she,' I suggested, 'and sits on the rock at the entrance, combing her hair?'

I wanted to draw him out, for I was interested in his sudden gravity, and there was a suggestion of irony in his last remark that puzzled me.

'Have you ever seen her?' he asked.

'Often and often.'

'I, never.'

'But you have heard her sing?'

He put on his coat and said impatiently, 'How can she sing under the water? Who could? She sometimes tries, but nothing comes from her but great bubbles.'

'She should climb on to the rock.'

'How can she?' he cried again, quite angry. 'The priests have blessed the air, so she cannot breathe it, and blessed the rocks, so that she cannot sit on them. But the sea no man can bless, because it is too big and always changing. So she lives in the sea.'

I was silent.

At this his face took a gentler expression. He looked at me as though something was on his mind, and going out to the entrance rock gazed at the external blue, then returning into our twilight he said, 'As a rule only good people see the Siren.'

I made no comment. There was a pause, and he continued. 'That is a very strange thing, and the priests do not know how to account for it; for she of course is wicked. Not only those who fast and go to Mass are in danger, but even those who are merely good in daily life. No one in the village had seen her for two generations. I am not surprised. We all cross ourselves before we enter the water, but it is unnecessary. Giuseppe, we thought, was safer than most. We loved him, and many of us he loved: but that is a different thing from being good.'

I asked who Giuseppe was.

'That day—I was seventeen and my brother was twenty and a great deal stronger than I was, and it was the year when the visitors, who have brought such prosperity and so many alterations into the village, first began to come. One English lady in particular, of very high birth, came, and has written a book

[1] a woodcut: a print made from an engraved wooden block.

about the place, and it was through her that the Improvement Syndicate was formed, which is about to connect the hotels with the station by a funicular railway.'

'Don't tell me about that lady in here,' I observed.

'That day we took her and her friends to see the grottoes. As we rowed close under the cliffs I put out my hand, as one does, and caught a little crab, and having pulled off its claws offered it as a curiosity. The ladies groaned, but a gentleman was pleased, and held out money. Being inexperienced, I refused it, saying that his pleasure was sufficient reward! Giuseppe, who 10 was rowing behind, was very angry with me and reached out with his hand and hit me on the side of the mouth, so that a tooth cut my lip and I bled. I tried to hit him back, but he always was too quick for me, and as I stretched round he kicked me under the armpit, so that for a moment I could not even row. There was a great noise among the ladies, and I heard afterwards that they were planning to take me away from my brother and train me as a waiter. That, at all events, never came to pass.

'When we reached the grotto—not here, but a larger one— the gentleman was very anxious that one of us should dive for 20 money, and the ladies consented, as they sometimes do. Giuseppe, who had discovered how much pleasure it gives foreigners to see us in the water, refused to dive for anything but silver, and the gentleman threw in a two-lira piece.

'Just before my brother sprang off he caught sight of me holding my bruise, and crying, for I could not help it. He laughed and said, "This time, at all events, I shall not see the Siren!" and went into the water without crossing himself. But he saw her.'

He broke off and accepted a cigarette. I watched the golden 30 entrance rock and the quivering walls and the magic water through which great bubbles constantly rose.

At last he dropped his hot ash into the ripples and turned his head away and said, 'He came up without the coin. We pulled him into the boat, and he was so large that he seemed to fill it, and so wet that we could not dress him. I have never seen a man so wet. I and the gentleman rowed back, and we covered Giuseppe with sacking and propped him up in the stern.'[1]

'He was drowned, then?' I murmured, supposing that to be the point.   40

'He was not,' he cried angrily. 'He saw the Siren. I told you.'

[1] stern: the back of a boat.

29

I was silenced again.

'We put him to bed though he was not ill. The doctor came and took money, and the priest came and spattered him with holy water. But it was no good. He was too big—like a piece of the sea. He kissed the thumb-bones of San Biagio[1] and they never dried till evening.'

'What did he look like?' I ventured.

'Like anyone who has seen the Siren. If you have seen her "often and often", how is it you do not know? Unhappy, unhappy because he knew everything. Every living thing made him unhappy because he knew it would die. And all he cared to do was sleep.'

I bent over my notebook.

'He did no work, he forgot to eat, he forgot whether he had his clothes on. All the work fell on me, and my sister had to go out to service. We tried to make him into a beggar, but he was too robust to inspire pity, and as for an idiot, he had not the right look in his eyes. He would stand in the street looking at people, and the more he looked at them the more unhappy he became. When a child was born he would cover his face with his hands. If anyone was married—he was terrible then, and would frighten them as they came out of church. Who would have believed he would marry himself! I caused that, I. I was reading out of the paper how a girl at Ragusa[2] had "gone mad through bathing in the sea". Giuseppe got up, and in a week he and that girl came in.

'He never told me anything, but it seems that he went straight to her house, broke into her room, and carried her off. She was the daughter of a rich mine-owner, so you may imagine our peril. Her father came down, with a clever lawyer, but they could do no more than I. They argued and they threatened, but at last they had to go back and we lost nothing—that is to say, no money. We took Giuseppe and Maria to the church and had them married. Ugh![3] that wedding! The priest made no jokes afterwards, and coming out the children threw stones. . . . I think I would have died to make her happy; but as always happens, one could do nothing.'

[1] San Biagio: St. Blaise who was a bishop in Armenia in the fourth century. The thumb bones are probably relics preserved on Capri. Giuseppe kisses them in the hope of getting better.

[2] Ragusa: a town in the South East of Sicily.

[3] Ugh!: an exclamation of horror.

'Were they unhappy together, then?'

'They loved each other, but love is not happiness. We can all get love. Love is nothing. I had two people to work for now, for she was like him in everything—one never knew which of them was speaking. I had to sell our own boat and work under the bad old man you have to-day. Worst of all, people began to hate us. The children first—everything begins with them—and then the women and last of all the men. For the cause of every misfortune was—you will not betray me?'

I promised good faith, and immediately he burst into the frantic blasphemy of one who has escaped from supervision, cursing the priests, who had ruined his life, he said. 'Thus are we tricked!' was his cry, and he stood up and kicked at the azure ripples with his feet, till he had obscured them with a cloud of sand.

I too was moved. The story of Giuseppe, for all its absurdity and superstition, came nearer to reality than anything I had known before. I don't know why, but it filled me with desire to help others—the greatest of all our desires, I suppose, and the most fruitless. The desire soon passed.

'She was about to have a child. That was the end of everything. People said to me, "When will your charming nephew be born? What a cheerful, attractive child he will be, with such a father and mother!" I kept my face steady and replied, "I think he may be. Out of sadness shall come gladness"—it is one of our proverbs. And my answer frightened them very much, and they told the priests, who were frightened too. Then the whisper started that the child would be Antichrist.[1] You need not be afraid: he was never born.

'An old witch began to prophesy, and no one stopped her. Giuseppe and the girl, she said, had silent devils, who could do little harm. But the child would always be speaking and laughing and perverting, and last of all he would go into the sea and fetch up the Siren into the air, and all the world would see her and hear her sing. As soon as she sang, the Seven Vials[2] would be opened and the Pope would die and Mongibello flame,[3] and the

[1] Antichrist: the title of a great personal opponent of Christ and his kingdom, expected by the early Church to appear before the end of the world.

[2] the Seven Vials: the bottles containing the anger of God which the angels poured on the earth.

[3] Mongibello flame: a local Sicilian name for the volcano Mount Etna.

31

veil of Santa Agata[1] would be burned. Then the boy and the Siren would marry, and together they would rule the world, for ever and ever.

'The whole village was in tumult, and the hotel-keepers became alarmed, for the tourist season was just beginning. They met together and decided that Giuseppe and the girl must be sent inland until the child was born, and they subscribed the money. The night before they were to start there was a full moon and wind from the east, and all along the coast the sea shot up over the cliffs in silver clouds. It is a wonderful sight, and Maria said she must see it once more.

' "Do not go," I said. "I saw the priest go by, and someone with him. And the hotel-keepers do not like you to be seen, and if we displease them also we shall starve."

' "I want to go," she replied. "The sea is stormy, and I may never feel it again."

' "No, he is right," said Giuseppe. "Do not go—or let one of us go with you."

' "I want to go alone," she said; and she went alone.

'I tied up their luggage in a piece of cloth, and then I was so unhappy at thinking I should lose them that I went and sat down by my brother and put my arm round his neck, and he put his arm round me, which he had not done for more than a year, and we remained thus I don't remember how long.

'Suddenly the door flew open and moonlight and wind came in together, and a child's voice said laughing. "They have pushed her over the cliffs into the sea."

'I stepped to the drawer where I keep my knives.

' "Sit down again," said Giuseppe—Giuseppe of all people! "If she is dead, why should others die too?"

' "I guess who it is," I cried, "and I will kill him."

'I was almost out of the door, and he tripped me up and, kneeling upon me, took hold of both my hands and sprained my wrists; first my right one, then my left. No one but Giuseppe would have thought of such a thing. It hurt more than you would suppose, and I fainted. When I woke up, he was gone, and I never saw him again.'

But Giuseppe disgusted me.

'I told you he was wicked,' he said. 'No one would have expected him to see the Siren.'

[1] Santa Agata: a virgin martyr in Sicily probably third century, and the patron saint of bell founders.

'How do you know he did see her?'

'Because he did not see her "often and often", but once.'

'Why do you love him if he is wicked?'

He laughed for the first time. That was his only reply.

'Is that the end?' I asked.

'I never killed her murderer, for by the time my wrists were well he was in America; and one cannot kill a priest. As for Giuseppe, he went all over the world too, looking for someone else who had seen the Siren—either a man or better still, a woman, for then the child might still have been born. At last he 10 came to Liverpool[1]—is the district probable?—and there he began to cough, and spat blood until he died.

'I do not suppose there is anyone living now who has seen her. There has seldom been more than one in a generation, and never in my life will there be both a man and a woman from whom that child can be born, who will fetch up the Siren from the sea, and destroy silence, and save the world!'

'Save the world?' I cried. 'Did the prophecy end like that?'

He leaned back against the rock, breathing deep. Through all the blue-green reflections I saw him colour. I heard him say: 20 'Silence and loneliness cannot last for ever. It may be a hundred or a thousand years, but the sea lasts longer, and she shall come out of it and sing.' I would have asked him more, but at that moment the whole cave darkened, and there rode in through its narrow entrance the returning boat.

Useful Phrases

1 All the same (page 26, line 23)—nevertheless, or in spite of what has happened.

2 to fall into the key of (page 27, line 27)—to adapt to what one's environment suggests is the appropriate mood.

3 to draw someone out (page 28, line 6)—to encourage someone to talk.

4 to have something on one's mind (page 28, line 24)—to be troubled or confused by something.

5 As a rule (page 28, line 26)—generally speaking, in general.

6 to account for something (page 28, line 29)—to be able to explain satisfactorily.

[1] Liverpool: a large port in the north-west of England.

33

7 to come to pass (page 29, line 18)—to happen or take place.
8 to break off (page 29, line 30)—to stop talking abruptly.
9 to care to do something (page 30, line 11)—to want to do.

Questions to guide the reader and also for further discussion or essay writing

1 Explain carefully what the author is trying to express in the following quotations:
a 'But it reappeared, quite sane though a little tremulous,' (page 26, lines 9 & 10).
b 'warbled the chaplain,' (page 26, line 16).
c '—cleanliness passed from the domestic to the sublime,' (page 26, lines 35 & 36).
d 'The children first—everything begins with them—' (page 31, line 7).
e 'and all along the coast the sea shot up and over the cliffs in silver clouds' (page 32, lines 9 & 10).
f 'Suddenly the door flew open and moonlight and wind came in together,' (page 32, lines 25 & 26).
g 'Through all the blue-green reflections I saw him colour' (page 33, lines 19 & 20).

2 Write brief sketches of the two brothers particularly trying to suggest any differences between them.

3 What evidence is there in the story of social criticism or the evil nature of progress?

4 What importance do (*a*) the sea, and (*b*) the village and its inhabitants play in the story?

5 'Here only the fantastic would be tolerable,' (page 27, lines 31 & 32). How far is this story a plea for such a world, removed from 'the commonplaces that are called reality'? (page 27, line 29).

6 'Don't tell me about that lady in here,' (page 29, line 4). Why does the narrator say this, and how would you answer the question he later asks the Sicilian about his brother Giuseppe—namely: 'Why do you love him if he is wicked?' (page 33, line 3).

7 '. . . desire to help others—the greatest of all our desires, I suppose, and the most fruitless' (page 31, lines 18-20). How far do you agree with this statement?

GRAHAM GREENE

The End of the Party

GRAHAM GREENE was born in 1904 and
educated first at Berkhamsted where his
father was headmaster, and later at Balliol
College, Oxford. While still at University he
had a book of verse published and afterwards
became a sub-editor of *The Times*. In 1926 he
was converted to Roman Catholicism, and his
first novel—*The Man Within*—appeared three
years later.

In 1935 he visited Liberia; he later went to
Mexico, and subsequently wrote a number of
books based on these journeys. On his return
to England he worked first as film critic and
later as the literary editor for the *Spectator*.
During the Second World War he worked for
the Foreign Office, and is now a director of
a London publishing firm.

He is one of the best of contemporary
English novelists and is also well known for
his short stories and plays.

Peter Morton woke with a start[1] to face the first light. Through the window he could see a bare bough dropping across a frame of silver. Rain tapped against the glass. It was January the fifth.

He looked across a table, on which a night-light[2] had guttered into a pool of water, at the other bed. Francis Morton was still asleep, and Peter lay down again with his eyes on his brother. It amused him to imagine that it was himself whom he watched, the same hair, the same eyes, the same lips and line of cheek. But the thought soon palled, and the mind went back to the fact which lent the day importance. It was the fifth of January. He could hardly believe that a year had passed since Mrs. Henne-Falcon had given her last children's party.

Francis turned suddenly upon his back and threw an arm across his face, blocking his mouth. Peter's heart began to beat fast, not with pleasure now but with uneasiness. He sat up and called across the table, 'Wake up.' Francis's shoulders shook and he waved a clenched fist in the air, but his eyes remained closed. To Peter Morton the whole room seemed suddenly to darken, and he had the impression of a great bird swooping. He cried again, 'Wake up,' and once more there was silver light and the touch of rain on the windows. Francis rubbed his eyes. 'Did you call out?' he asked.

'You are having a bad dream,' Peter said with confidence. Already experience had taught him how far their minds reflected each other. But he was the elder, by a matter of minutes, and that brief extra interval of light, while his brother still struggled in pain and darkness, had given him self-reliance and an instinct of protection towards the other who was afraid of so many things.

'I dreamed that I was dead,' Francis said.

'What was it like?' Peter asked with curiosity.

'I can't remember,' Francis said, and his eyes turned with relief to the silver of day, as he allowed the fragmentary memories to fade.

'You dreamed of a big bird.'

'Did I?' Francis accepted his brother's knowledge without question, and for a little the two lay silent in bed facing each other, the same green eyes, the same nose tilting at the tip, the

---

[1] with a start: suddenly.

[2] a night-light: a small, slow-burning candle, which stands in a saucer of water and is left to burn in a child's bedroom.

36

same firm lips parted, and the same premature modelling of the chin. The fifth of January, Peter thought again, his mind drifting idly from the image of cakes to the prizes which might be won. Egg-and-spoon races, spearing apples in basins of water, blind man's buff.[1]

'I don't want to go,' Francis said suddenly. 'I suppose Joyce will be there . . . Mabel Warren.' Hateful to him, the thought of a party shared with those two. They were older than he. Joyce was eleven and Mabel Warren thirteen. Their long pigtails[2] swung superciliously to a masculine stride. Their sex humiliated him, as they watched him fumble with his egg,[3] from under lowered scornful lids. And last year . . . he turned his face away from Peter, his cheeks scarlet.

'What's the matter?' Peter asked.

'Oh, nothing. I don't think I'm well. I've got a cold. I oughtn't to go to the party.' Peter was puzzled. 'But, Francis, is it a bad cold?'

'It will be a bad cold if I go to the party. Perhaps I shall die.'

'Then you mustn't go,' Peter said with decision, prepared to solve all difficulties with one plain sentence, and Francis let his nerves relax in a delicious relief, ready to leave everything to Peter. But though he was grateful he did not turn his face towards his brother. His cheeks still bore the badge of a shameful memory, of the game of hide and seek last year in the darkened house, and of how he had screamed when Mabel Warren put her hand suddenly upon his arm. He had not heard her coming. Girls were like that. Their shoes never squeaked. No boards whined under their tread. They slunk like cats on padded claws.

When the nurse came in with hot water Francis lay tranquil leaving everything to Peter. Peter said, 'Nurse, Francis has got a cold.'

The tall starched woman laid the towels across the cans and said, without turning, 'The washing won't be back till tomorrow. You must lend him some of your handkerchiefs.'

'But, Nurse,' Peter asked, 'hadn't he better stay in bed?'

'We'll take him for a good walk this morning,' the nurse said.

[1] blind man's buff: a game in which one person is blindfolded and tries to catch the others.

[2] pigtails: hair plaited so as to hang behind the head.

[3] 'they watched him fumble with his egg,': this refers to the egg-and-spoon races.

37

'Wind'll blow away the germs. Get up now, both of you,' and she closed the door behind her.

'I'm sorry,' Peter said, and then, worried at the sight of a face creased again by misery and foreboding, 'Why don't you just stay in bed? I'll tell mother you felt too ill to get up.' But such a rebellion against destiny was not in Francis's power. Besides, if he stayed in bed they would come up and tap his chest and put a thermometer in his mouth and look at his tongue, and they would discover that he was malingering. It was true that he felt ill, a sick empty sensation in his stomach and a rapidly beating heart, but he knew that the cause was only fear, fear of the party, fear of being made to hide by himself in the dark, uncompanioned by Peter and with no night-light to make a blessed breach.

'No, I'll get up,' he said, and then with sudden desperation, 'But I won't go to Mrs. Henne-Falcon's party. I swear on the Bible I won't.' Now surely all would be well, he thought. God would not allow him to break so solemn an oath. He would show him a way. There was all the morning before him and all the afternoon until four o'clock. No need to worry now when the grass was still crisp with the early frost. Anything might happen. He might cut himself or break his leg or really catch a bad cold. God would manage somehow.

He had such confidence in God that when at breakfast his mother said, 'I hear you have a cold, Francis,' he made light of it. 'We should have heard more about it,' his mother said with irony, 'if there was not a party this evening,' and Francis smiled uneasily, amazed and daunted by her ignorance of him. His happiness would have lasted longer if, out for a walk that morning, he had not met Joyce. He was alone with his nurse, for Peter had leave to finish a rabbit-hutch in the wood-shed. If Peter had been there he would have cared less; the nurse was Peter's nurse also, but now it was as though she was employed only for his sake, because he could not be trusted to go for a walk alone. Joyce was only two years older and she was by herself.

She came striding towards them, pigtails flapping. She glanced scornfully at Francis and spoke with ostentation to the nurse. 'Hello, Nurse. Are you bringing Francis to the party this evening? Mabel and I are coming.' And she was off again down the street in the direction of Mabel Warren's home, consciously alone and self-sufficient in the long empty road. 'Such a nice girl,' the nurse said. But Francis was silent, feeling again the jump-jump of his heart, realising how soon the hour of the party would arrive. God had done nothing for him, and the minutes flew.

They flew too quickly to plan any evasion, or even to prepare his heart for the coming ordeal. Panic nearly overcame him when, all unready, he found himself standing on the doorstep, with coat-collar turned up against a cold wind, and the nurse's electric torch making a short luminous trail through the darkness. Behind him were the lights of the hall and the sound of a servant laying the table for dinner, which his mother and father 10 would eat alone. He was nearly overcome by a desire to run back into the house and call out to his mother that he would not go to the party, that he dared not go. They could not make him go. He could almost hear himself saying those final words, breaking down for ever, as he knew instinctively, the barrier of ignorance that saved his mind from his parents' knowledge. 'I'm afraid of going. I won't go. I daren't go. They'll make me hide in the dark, and I'm afraid of the dark. I'll scream and scream and scream.' He could see the expression of amazement on his mother's face, and then the cold confidence of a grown-up's retort. 20

'Don't be silly. You must go. We've accepted Mrs. Henne-Falcon's invitation.' But they couldn't make him go; hesitating on the doorstep while the nurse's feet crunched across the frost-covered grass to the gate, he knew that. He would answer: 'You can say I'm ill. I won't go. I'm afraid of the dark.' And his mother: 'Don't be silly. You know there's nothing to be afraid of in the dark.' But he knew the falsity of that reasoning; he knew how they taught also that there was nothing to fear in death, and how fearfully they avoided the idea of it. But they couldn't make him go to the party. 'I'll scream. I'll scream.' 30

'Francis, come along.' He heard the nurse's voice across the dimly phosphorescent lawn and saw the small yellow circle of her torch wheel from tree to shrub and back to tree again. 'I'm coming,' he called with despair, leaving the lighted doorway of the house; he couldn't bring himself to lay bare his last secrets and end reserve between his mother and himself, for there was still in the last resort a further appeal possible to Mrs. Henne-Falcon. He comforted himself with that, as he advanced steadily across the hall, very small, towards her enormous bulk. His heart beat unevenly, but he had control now over his voice, as 40 he said with meticulous accent, 'Good evening, Mrs. Henne-Falcon. It was very good of you to ask me to your party.' With

39

his strained face lifted towards the curve of her breasts, and his polite set speech, he was like an old withered man. For Francis mixed very little with other children. As a twin he was in many ways an only child. To address Peter was to speak to his own image in a mirror, an image a little altered by a flaw in the glass, so as to throw back less a likeness of what he was than of what he wished to be, what he would be without his unreasoning fear of darkness, foot-steps of strangers, the flights of bats in dusk-filled gardens.

'Sweet child,' said Mrs. Henne-Falcon absent-mindedly, be- 10 fore, with a wave of her arms, as though the children were a flock of chickens, she whirled them into her set programme of entertainments: egg-and-spoon races, three-legged races, the spearing of apples, games which held for Francis nothing worse than humiliation. And in the frequent intervals when nothing was required of him and he could stand alone in corners as far removed as possible from Mabel Warren's scornful gaze, he was able to plan how he might avoid the approaching terror of the dark. He knew there was nothing to fear until after tea, and not until he was sitting down in a pool of yellow radiance 20 cast by the ten candles on Colin Henne-Falcon's birthday cake did he become fully conscious of the imminence of what he feared. Through the confusion of his brain, now assailed suddenly by a dozen contradictory plans, he heard Joyce's high voice down the table. 'After tea we are going to play hide and seek in the dark.'

'Oh, no,' Peter said, watching Francis's troubled face with pity and an imperfect understanding, 'don't let's. We play that every year.'

'But it's in the programme,' cried Mabel Warren. 'I saw it 30 myself. I looked over Mrs. Henne-Falcon's shoulder. Five o'clock, tea. A quarter to six to half-past, hide and seek in the dark. It's all written down in the programme.'

Peter did not argue, for if hide and seek had been inserted in Mrs. Henne-Falcon's programme, nothing which he could say would avert it. He asked for another piece of birthday cake and sipped his tea slowly. Perhaps it might be possible to delay the game for a quarter of an hour, allow Francis at least a few extra minutes to form a plan, but even in that Peter failed, for children were already leaving the table in twos and threes. It 40 was his third failure, and again, the reflection of an image in another's mind, he saw a great bird darken his brother's face with its wings. But he upbraided himself silently for his folly, and finished his cake encouraged by the memory of that adult refrain, 'There's nothing to fear in the dark.' The last to leave the table, the brothers came together to the hall to meet the mustering and impatient eyes of Mrs. Henne-Falcon.

'And now,' she said, 'we will play hide and seek in the dark.'

Peter watched his brother and saw, as he had expected, the lips tighten. Francis, he knew, had feared this moment from the beginning of the party, had tried to meet it with courage and had abandoned the attempt. He must have prayed desperately 10 for cunning to evade the game, which was now welcomed with cries of excitement by all the other children. 'Oh, do let's.' 'We must pick sides.' 'Is any of the house out of bounds?' 'Where shall home¹ be?'

'I think,' said Francis Morton, approaching Mrs. Henne-Falcon, his eyes focused unwaveringly on her exuberant breasts, 'it will be no use my playing. My nurse will be calling for me very soon.'

'Oh, but your nurse can wait, Francis,' said Mrs. Henne-Falcon absent-mindedly, while she clapped her hands together to 20 summon to her side a few children who were already straying up the wide staircase to upper floors. 'Your mother will never mind.'

That had been the limit of Francis's cunning. He had refused to believe that so well-prepared an excuse could fail. All that he could say now, still in the precise tone which other children hated, thinking it a symbol of conceit, was, 'I think I had better not play.' He stood motionless, retaining, though afraid, unmoved features. But the knowledge of his terror, or the reflection of the terror itself, reached his brother's brain. For the moment, 30 Peter Morton could have cried aloud with the fear of bright lights going out, leaving him alone in an island of dark surrounded by the gentle lapping of strange foot-steps. Then he remembered that the fear was not his own, but his brother's. He said impulsively to Mrs. Henne-Falcon, 'Please, I don't think Francis should play. The dark makes him jump so.' They were the wrong words. Six children began to sing, 'Cowardy cowardy custard,'² turning torturing faces with the vacancy of wide sunflowers towards Francis Morton.

¹ home: the place to reach or return to at the end of a game.

² Cowardy cowardy custard: a phrase used by children to indicate cowardice.

41

Without looking at his brother, Francis said, 'Of course I'll play. I'm not afraid, I only thought . . .' But he was already forgotten by his human tormentors and was able in loneliness to contemplate the approach of the spiritual, the more unbounded torture. The children scrambled round Mrs. Henne-Falcon, their shrill voices pecking at her with questions and suggestions. 'Yes, anywhere in the house. We will turn out all the lights. Yes, you can hide in the cupboards. You must stay hidden as long as you can. There will be no home.'

Peter, too, stood apart, ashamed of the clumsy manner in   10
which he had tried to help his brother. Now he could feel, creeping in at the corners of his brain, all Francis's resentment of his championing. Several children ran upstairs, and the lights on the top floor went out. Then darkness came down like the wings of a bat and settled on the landing.[1] Others began to put out the lights at the edge of the hall, till the children were all gathered in the central radiance of the chandelier, while the bats squatted round on hooded wings and waited for that, too, to be extinguished.

'You and Francis are on the hiding side,' a tall girl said, and   20
then the light was gone, and the carpet wavered under his feet with the sibilance of footfalls, like small cold draughts, creeping away into corners.

'Where's Francis?' he wondered. 'If I join him he'll be less frightened of all these sounds.' 'These sounds' were the casing of silence: the squeak of a loose board, the cautious closing of a cupboard door, the whine of a finger drawn along polished wood.

Peter stood in the centre of the dark deserted floor, not listening but waiting for the idea of his brother's whereabouts   30
to enter his brain. But Francis crouched with fingers on his ears, eyes uselessly closed, mind numbed against impressions, and only a sense of strain could cross the gap of dark. Then a voice called 'Coming', and as though his brother's self-possession had been shattered by the sudden cry, Peter Morton jumped with his fear. But it was not his own fear. What in his brother was a burning panic, admitting no ideas except those which added to the flame, was in him an altruistic emotion that left the reason unimpaired. 'Where, if I were Francis, should I hide?' Such, roughly, was his thought. And because he was, if not Francis   40
himself, at least a mirror to him, the answer was immediate.

[1] landing: the level part of a staircase between the flights of stairs.

42

'Between the oak bookcase on the left of the study door, and the leather settee.' Peter Morton was unsurprised by the swiftness of the response. Between the twins there could be no jargon of telepathy. They had been together in the womb, and they could not be parted.

Peter Morton tiptoed towards Francis's hiding place. Occasionally a board rattled, and because he feared to be caught by one of the soft questers through the dark, he bent and untied his laces. A tag struck the floor and the metallic sound set a host of cautious feet moving in his direction. But by that time he was 10 in his stockings and would have laughed inwardly at the pursuit had not the noise of someone stumbling on his abandoned shoes made his heart trip in the reflection of another's surprise. No more boards revealed Peter Morton's progress. On stockinged feet he moved silently and unerringly towards his object. Instinct told him that he was near the wall, and, extending a hand, he laid the fingers across his brother's face.

Francis did not cry out, but the leap of his own heart revealed to Peter a proportion of Francis's terror. 'It's all right,' he whispered, feeling down the squatting figure until he captured a 20 clenched hand. 'It's only me. I'll stay with you.' And grasping the other tightly, he listened to the cascade of whispers his utterance had caused to fall. A hand touched the bookcase close to Peter's head and he was aware of how Francis's fear continued in spite of his presence. It was less intense, more bearable, he hoped, but it remained. He knew that it was his brother's fear and not his own that he experienced. The dark to him was only an absence of light; the groping hand that of a familiar child. Patiently he waited to be found.

He did not speak again, for between Francis and himself touch 30 was the most intimate communion. By way of joined hands thought could flow more swiftly than lips could shape themselves round words. He could experience the whole progress of his brother's emotion, from the leap of panic at the unexpected contact to the steady pulse of fear, which now went on and on with the regularity of a heart-beat. Peter Morton thought with intensity, 'I am here. You needn't be afraid. The lights will go on again soon. That rustle, that movement is nothing to fear. Only Joyce, only Mabel Warren.' He bombarded the drooping form with thoughts of safety, but he was conscious that the fear 40 continued. 'They are beginning to whisper together. They are tired of looking for us. The lights will go on soon. We shall have

43

won. Don't be afraid. That was only someone on the stairs. I believe it's Mrs. Henne-Falcon. Listen. They are feeling for the lights.' Feet moving on a carpet, hands brushing a wall, a curtain pulled apart, a clicking handle, the opening of a cupboard door. In the case above their heads a loose book shifted under a touch. 'Only Joyce, only Mabel Warren, only Mrs. Henne-Falcon,' a crescendo of reassuring thought before the chandelier burst, like a fruit tree, into bloom.

The voices of the children rose shrilly into the radiance. 'Where's Peter?' 'Have you looked upstairs?' 'Where's Francis?' 10 but they were silenced again by Mrs. Henne-Falcon's scream. But she was not the first to notice Francis Morton's stillness, where he had collapsed against the wall at the touch of his brother's hand. Peter continued to hold the clenched fingers in an arid and puzzled grief. It was not merely that his brother was dead. His brain, too young to realize the full paradox, yet wondered with an obscure self-pity why it was that the pulse of his brother's fear went on and on, when Francis was now where he had been always told there was no more terror and no more darkness.

Useful Phrases

1 to make light of (page 38, line 25)—to minimize the importance.
2 to have leave to (page 38, line 31)—to have permission.
3 to break down (page 39, lines 14 & 15)—to collapse in an emotional sense.
4 to bring onself (page 39, line 35)—to persuade or force oneself.
5 to lay bare (page 39, line 35)—to expose, reveal.
6 the last resort (page 39, line 37)—the final action one can take in an emergency when all else has failed.
7 out of bounds (page 41, line 13)—an area one is not allowed to enter.
8 to call for (page 41, line 17)—to collect.
9 a host of (page 43, line 9)—a large number.

Questions to guide the reader and also for further discussion or essay writing

1 Explain carefully what the author is trying to express in the following quotations:
a 'the barrier of ignorance that saved his mind from his parents' knowledge' (page 39, lines 15 & 16).

b 'As a twin he was in many ways an only child' (page 40, lines 3 & 4).

c 'their shrill voices pecking at her with questions and suggestions' (page 42, line 6).

d 'while the bats squatted round on hooded wings and waited for that, too, to be extinguished' (page 42, lines 17–18).

e 'the noise of someone stumbling on his abandoned shoes made his heart trip in the reflection of another's surprise' (page 43, lines 12 & 13).

2 What is the main theme of this story? Are there subsidiary, yet important ones, as well?

3 Why does Francis finally join the game of hide and seek in the dark in spite of his fear of the dark?

4 What part do the various adults play in the story? Do you think they can be held at all responsible for Francis's death?

5 Comment upon the following quotation: 'he knew how they taught also that there was nothing to fear in death, and how fearfully they avoided the idea of it' (page 39, lines 27–29).

6 'He did not speak again, for between Francis and himself touch was the most intimate communion' (page 43, lines 30 & 31). What is the full significance of this quotation in the context of the whole story?

D. H. LAWRENCE

The Last Laugh

D. H. LAWRENCE, the son of a coal-miner,
was born in Nottinghamshire in 1885. He won
a scholarship to Nottingham High School and
later attended Nottingham University to
obtain a teacher's certificate. Subsequently he
taught at an elementary school until the
publication of his first book—*The White Peacock*
(1911)—made him decide to devote his time to
writing.

He married in 1914, and after spending the
First World War in England, travelled for
many years in different parts of the world.
After settling in New Mexico for a time, he
returned to Europe in 1929 and died in the
South of France in the following year.

Although his works gave rise to a great deal
of controversy during his lifetime, he is now
generally acknowledged to be one of the
greatest of English writers. His work includes
a considerable number of novels, short stories,
essays, literary criticism, and poems.

THERE WAS A little snow on the ground, and the church clock had just struck midnight. Hampstead[1] in the night of winter for once was looking pretty, with clean white earth and lamps for moon, and dark sky above the lamps.

A confused little sound of voices, a gleam of hidden yellow light. And then the garden door of a tall, dark Georgian house[2] suddenly opened, and three people confusedly emerged. A girl in a dark blue coat and fur turban, very erect: a fellow with a little dispatch-case, slouching: a thin man with a red beard, bareheaded, peering out of the gateway down the hill that 10 swung in a curve downwards towards London.

'Look at it! A new world!' cried the man in the beard, ironically, as he stood on the step and peered out.

'No, Lorenzo! It's only whitewash!' cried the young man in the overcoat. His voice was handsome, resonant, plangent, with a weary sardonic touch. As he turned back his face was dark in shadow.

The girl with the erect, alert head, like a bird, turned back to the two men.

'What was that?' she asked, in her quick, quiet voice. 20

'Lorenzo says it's a new world. I say it's only whitewash,' cried the man in the street.

She stood still and lifted her woolly, gloved finger. She was deaf and was taking it in.

Yes, she had got it. She gave a quick, chuckling laugh, glanced very quickly at the man in the bowler hat, then back at the man in the stucco gateway, who was grinning like a satyr and waving good-bye.

'Good-bye, Lorenzo!' came the resonant, weary cry of the man in the bowler hat. 30

'Good-bye!' came the sharp, night-bird call of the girl.

The green gate slammed, then the inner door. The two were alone in the street, save for[3] the policeman at the corner. The road curved steeply downhill.

'You'd better mind how you *step*!' shouted the man in the bowler hat, leaning near the erect, sharp girl, and slouching in his walk. She paused a moment to make sure what he had said.

'Don't mind me, I'm quite all right. Mind yourself!' she said

[1] Hampstead: a fashionable London suburb.
[2] Georgian house: a house built in the English architectural style of the period 1700–1830.
[3] save for: except, apart from.

47

quickly. At that very moment he gave a wild lurch on the slippery snow, but managed to save himself from falling. She watched him, on tiptoes of alertness. His bowler hat bounced away in the thin snow. They were under a lamp near the curve. As he ducked for his hat he showed a bald spot, just like a tonsure, among his dark, thin, rather curly hair. And when he looked up at her, with his thick black brows sardonically arched, and his rather hooked nose self-derisive, jamming his hat on again, he seemed like a satanic young priest. His face had beautiful lines, like a faun, and a doubtful martyred expression. A sort of faun on the Cross, with all the malice of the complication.

'Did you hurt yourself?' she asked, in her quick, cool, unemotional way.

'No!' he shouted derisively.

'Give me the machine, won't you?' she said, holding out her woolly hand. 'I believe I'm safer.'

'Do you *want* it?' he shouted.

'Yes, I'm sure I'm safer.'

He handed her the little brown dispatch-case, which was really a Marconi listening machine for her deafness. She marched erect as ever. He shoved his hands deep in his overcoat pockets and slouched along beside her, as if he wouldn't make his legs firm. The road curved down in front of them, clean and pale with snow under the lamps. A motor-car came churning up. A few dark figures slipped away into the dark recesses of the houses, like fishes among rocks above a sea bed of white sand. On the left was a tuft of trees sloping upwards into the dark.

He kept looking around, pushing out his finely shaped chin and his hooked nose as if he were listening for something. He could still hear the motor-car climbing on to the Heath.[1] Below was the yellow, foul-smelling glare of the Hampstead Tube station.[2] On the right the trees.

The girl, with her alert pink-and-white face, looked at him sharply, inquisitively. She had an odd nymph-like inquisitiveness, sometimes like a bird, sometimes a squirrel, sometimes a rabbit: never quite like a woman. At last he stood still, as if he would go no farther. There was a curious, baffled grin on his smooth, cream-coloured face.

[1] Heath: Hampstead Heath, the open parkland of the suburb.
[2] Tube station: the underground railway station.

'James,' he said loudly to her, leaning towards her ear. 'Do you hear somebody *laughing*?'

'Laughing?' she retorted quickly. 'Who's laughing?'

'I don't know. *Somebody!*' he shouted, showing his teeth at her in a very odd way.

'No, I hear nobody,' she announced.

'But it's most *extraordinary*!' he cried, his voice slurring up and down. 'Put on your machine.'

'Put it on?' she retorted. 'What for?'

'To see if you can *hear* it,' he cried.   10

'Hear what?'

'The *laughing*. Somebody laughing. It's most *extraordinary*.'

She gave her odd little chuckle and handed him her machine. He held it while she opened the lid and attached the wires, putting the band over her head and the receivers at her ears, like a wireless operator. Crumbs of snow fell down the cold darkness. She switched on: little yellow lights in glass tubes shone in the machine. She was connected, she was listening. He stood with his head ducked, his hands shoved down in his over-coat pockets.   20

Suddenly he lifted his face and gave the weirdest, slightly neighing laugh, uncovering his strong spaced teeth and arching his black brows, and watching her with queer, gleaming, goat-like eyes.

She seemed a little dismayed.

'There!' he said. 'Didn't you hear it?'

'I heard *you*,' she said, in a tone which conveyed that *that* was enough.

'But didn't you hear *it*?' he cried, unfurling his lips oddly again.   30

'No!' she said.

He looked at her vindictively, and stood again with ducked head. She remained erect, her fur hat in her hand, her fine bobbed hair banded with the machine-band and catching crumbs of snow, her odd, bright-eyed, deaf nymph's face lifted with blank listening.

'There!' he cried, suddenly perking up his gleaming face. 'You mean to tell me you can't—' He was looking at her almost diabolically. But something else was too strong for him. His face wreathed with a startling, peculiar smile, seeming to gleam, and 40 suddenly the most extraordinary laugh came bursting out of him, like an animal laughing. It was a strange neighing sound, amazing in her ears. She was startled, and switched her machine quieter.

A large form loomed up: a tall, clean-shaven young policeman.

'A radio?' he asked laconically.

'No, it's my machine. I'm deaf!' said Miss James quickly and distinctly. She was not the daughter of a peer[1] for nothing.

The man in the bowler hat lifted his face and glared at the fresh-faced young policeman with a peculiar white glare in his eyes.

'Look here!' he said distinctly. 'Did you hear someone 10 laughing?'

'Laughing? I heard you, sir.'

'No, *not* me.' He gave an impatient jerk of his arm, and lifted his face again. His smooth, creamy face seemed to gleam, there were subtle curves of derisive triumph in all its lines. He was careful not to look directly at the young policeman. 'The most extraordinary laughter I ever heard,' he added, and the same touch of derisive exultation sounded in his tones.

The policeman looked down on him cogitatingly.

'It's perfectly all right,' said Miss James coolly. 'He's not 20 drunk. He just hears something that we don't hear.'

'Drunk!' echoed the man in the bowler hat, in profoundly amused derision. 'If I were merely drunk—' And off he went again in the wild, neighing, animal laughter, while his averted face seemed to flash.

At the sound of the laughter something roused in the blood of the girl and of the policeman. They stood nearer to one another, so that their sleeves touched and they looked wonderingly across at the man in the bowler hat. He lifted his black brows at them.   30

'Do you mean to say you heard nothing?' he asked.

'Only you,' said Miss James.

'Only you, sir!' echoed the policeman.

'What was it like?' asked Miss James.

'Ask me to *describe* it!' retorted the young man, in extreme contempt. 'It's the most marvellous sound in the world.'

And truly he seemed wrapped up in a new mystery.

'Where does it come from?' asked Miss James, very practical.

'*Apparently*,' he answered in contempt, 'from over there.' And he pointed to the trees and bushes inside the railings over the 40 road.

[1] peer: a person entitled to sit in the House of Lords.

50

'Well, let's go and see!' she said. 'I can carry my machine and go on listening.'

The man seemed relieved to get rid of the burden. He shoved his hands in his pockets again and sloped off across the road. The policeman, a queer look flickering on his fresh young face, put his hand round the girl's arm carefully and subtly to help her. She did not lean at all on the support of the big hand, but she was interested, so she did not resent it. Having held herself all her life intensely aloof from physical contact, and never hav- ing let any man touch her, she now, with a certain nymph-like 10 voluptuousness, allowed the large hand of the young policeman to support her as they followed the quick wolf-like figure of the other man across the road uphill. And she could feel the presence of the young policeman, through all the thickness of his dark- blue uniform, as something young and alert and bright.

When they came up to the man in the bowler hat, he was standing with his head ducked, his ears pricked,[1] listening beside the iron rail inside which grew big black holly-trees tufted with snow, and old, ribbed, silent English elms. The policeman and the girl stood waiting. She was peering 20 into the bushes with the sharp eyes of a deaf nymph, deaf to the world's noises. The man in the bowler hat listened intensely. A lorry rolled downhill, making the earth tremble.

'There!' cried the girl, as the lorry rumbled darkly past. And she glanced round with flashing eyes at the policeman, her fresh soft face gleaming with startled life. She glanced straight into the puzzled, amused eyes of the young policeman. He was just enjoying himself.

'Don't you see?' she said, rather imperiously.

'What is it, Miss?' answered the policeman. 30

'I mustn't point,' she said. 'Look where I look.'

And she looked away with brilliant eyes, into the dark holly bushes. She must see something, for she smiled faintly, with subtle satisfaction, and she tossed her erect head in all the pride of vindication. The policeman looked at her instead of into the bushes. There was a certain brilliance of triumph and vindica- tion in all the poise of her slim body.

'I always knew I should see him,' she said triumphantly to herself.

'Whom do you see?' shouted the man in the bowler hat. 40

'Don't you see him too?' she asked, turning round her soft,

[1] pricked: listening alertly.

51

arch, nymph-like face anxiously. She was anxious for the little man to see.

'No, I see nothing. What do you see, James?' cried the man in the bowler hat, insisting.

'A man.'

'Where?'

'There. Among the holly bushes.'

'Is he there now?'

'No! He's gone.'

'What sort of a man?'   10

'I don't know.'

'What did he look like?'

'I can't tell you.'

But at that instant the man in the bowler hat turned sud-. denly, and the arch, triumphant look flew to his face.

'Why, he must be *there*!' he cried, pointing up the grove. 'Don't you hear him laughing? He must be behind those trees.'

And his voice, with curious delight, broke into a laugh again, as he stood and stamped his feet on the snow, and danced to his own laughter, ducking his head. Then he turned away and ran 20 swiftly up the avenue lined with old trees.

He slowed down as a door at the end of a garden path, white with untouched snow, suddenly opened, and a woman in a long-fringed shawl stood in the light. She peered out into the night. Then she came down to the low garden gate. Crumbs of snow still fell. She had dark hair and a tall dark comb.

'Did you knock at my door?' she asked of the man in the bowler hat.

'I? No!'

'Somebody knocked at my door.'   30

'Did they? Are you sure? They can't have done. There are no footmarks in the snow.'

'Nor are there!' she said. 'But somebody knocked and called something.'

'That's very curious,' said the man. 'Were you expecting someone?'

'No. Not exactly expecting anyone. Except that one is always expecting Somebody, you know.' In the dimness of the snow-lit night he could see her making big, dark eyes at him.

'Was it someone laughing?' he said.   40

'No. It was no one laughing, exactly. Someone knocked, and I ran to open, hoping as one always hopes, you know—'

'What?'

'Oh—that something wonderful is going to happen.'

He was standing close to the low gate. She stood on the opposite side. Her hair was dark, her face seemed dusky, as she looked up at him with her dark, meaningful eyes.

'Did you wish someone would come?' he asked.

'Very much,' she replied, in her plangent Jewish voice. She must be a Jewess.

'No matter who?' he said laughing.

'So long as it was a man I could like,' she said in a low, meaningful, falsely shy voice.

'Really!' he said. 'Perhaps after all it was I who knocked— without knowing.'

'I think it was,' she said. 'It must have been.'

'Shall I come in?' he asked, putting his hand on the little gate.

'Don't you think you'd better?' she replied.

He bent down, unlatching the gate. As he did so the woman in the black shawl turned, and glancing over her shoulder, hurried back to the house, walking unevenly in the snow, on her high-heeled shoes. The man hurried after her, hastening like a hound to catch up.

Meanwhile the girl and the policeman had come up. The girl stood still when she saw the man in the bowler hat going up the garden walk after the woman in the black shawl with the fringe.

'Is he going in?' she asked quickly.

'Looks like it, doesn't it?' said the policeman.

'Does he know that woman?'

'I can't say. I should say he soon will,' replied the policeman.

'But who is she?'

'I couldn't say who she is.'

The two dark, confused figures entered the lighted doorway, then the door closed on them.

'He's gone,' said the girl outside on the snow. She hastily began to pull off the band of her telephone-receiver, and switched off her machine. The tubes of secret light disappeared, she packed up the little leather case. Then, pulling on her soft fur cap, she stood once more ready.

The slightly martial look which her long, dark-blue, military-seeming coat gave her was intensified, while the slightly anxious, bewildered look on her face had gone. She seemed to stretch herself, to stretch her limbs free. And the inert look had left her full soft cheeks. Her cheeks were alive with the glimmer of pride and a new dangerous surety.

She looked quickly at the tall young policeman. He was clean-shaven, fresh-faced, smiling oddly under his helmet, waiting in subtle patience a few yards away. She saw that he was a decent young man, one of the waiting sort.

The second of ancient fear was followed at once in her by a blithe, unaccustomed sense of power.

'Well!' she said. 'I should say it's no use waiting.' She spoke 10 decisively.

'You don't have to wait for him, do you?' asked the policeman.

'Not at all. He's much better where he is.' She laughed an odd, brief laugh. Then glancing over her shoulder, she set off down the hill, carrying her little case. Her feet felt light, her legs felt long and strong. She glanced over her shoulder again. The young policeman was following her, and she laughed to herself. Her limbs felt so lithe and so strong, if she wished she could easily run faster than he. If she wished she could easily kill him, even with her hands. 20

So it seemed to her. But why kill him? He was a decent young fellow. She had in front of her eyes the dark face among the holly bushes, with the brilliant mocking eyes. Her breast felt full of power, and her legs felt long and strong and wild. She was surprised herself at the strong, bright, throbbing sensation beneath her breasts, a sensation of triumph and of rosy anger. Her hands felt keen on her wrists. She who had always declared she had not a muscle in her body! Even now, it was not muscle, it was a sort of flame.

Suddenly it began to snow heavily, with fierce frozen puffs of 30 wind. The snow was small, in frozen grains, and hit sharp on her face. It seemed to whirl round her as if she herself were whirling in a cloud. But she did not mind. There was a flame in her, her limbs felt flamey and strong, amid the whirl.

And the whirling, snowy air seemed full of presences,[1] full of strange unheard voices. She was used to the sensation of noises taking place which she could not hear. The sensation became very strong. She felt something was happening in the wild air.

The London air was no longer heavy and clammy, saturated with ghosts of the unwilling dead. A new, clean tempest swept 40 down from the Pole, and there were noises.

[1] presences: spirits.

Voices were calling. In spite of her deafness she could hear someone, several voices, calling and whistling, as if many people were hallooing through the air:

'He's come back! Aha! He's come back!'

There was a wild, whistling, jubilant sound of voices in the storm of snow. Then obscured lightning winked through the snow in the air.

'Is that thunder and lightning?' she asked of the young policeman, as she stood still, waiting for his form to emerge through the veil of whirling snow.

'Seems like it to me,' he said.

And at that very moment the lightning blinked again, and the dark, laughing face was near her face, it almost touched her cheek.

She started back, but a flame of delight went over her.

'There!' she said. 'Did you see that?'

'It lightened,' said the policeman.

She was looking at him almost angrily. But then the clean, fresh animal look of his skin, and the tame-animal look in his frightened eyes amused her, she laughed her low, triumphant laugh. He was obviously afraid, like a frightened dog that sees something uncanny.

The storm suddenly whistled louder, more violently, and, with a strange noise like castanets, she seemed to hear voices clapping and crying:

'He is here! He's come back!'

She nodded her head gravely.

The policeman and she moved on side by side. She lived alone in a little stucco house in a side street down the hill. There was a church and a grove of trees and then the little old row of houses. The wind blew fiercely, thick with snow. Now and again a taxi went by, with its lights showing weirdly. But the world seemed empty, uninhabited save by snow and voices.

As the girl and the policeman turned past the grove of trees near the church, a great whirl of wind and snow made them stand still, and in the wild confusion they heard a whirling of sharp, delighted voices, something like seagulls, crying:

'He's here! He's here!'

'Well, I'm jolly glad he's back,' said the girl calmly.

'What's that?' said the nervous policeman, hovering near the girl.

The wind let them move forward. As they passed along the railings it seemed to them the doors of the church were open, and the windows were out, and the snow and the voices were blowing in a wild career[1] all through the church.

'How extraordinary that they left the church open!' said the girl.

The policeman stood still. He could not reply.

As they stood they listened to the wind and the church full of whirling voices all calling confusedly.

'*Now* I hear the laughing,' she said suddenly.

It came from the church: a sound of low, subtle, endless laughter, a strange, naked sound.

'Now I hear it!' she said.

But the policeman did not speak. He stood cowed,[2] with his tail between his legs, listening to the strange noises in the church.

The wind must have blown out one of the windows, for they could see the snow whirling in volleys through the black gap, and whirling inside the church like a dim light. There came a sudden crash, followed by a burst of chuckling, naked laughter. The snow seemed to make a queer light inside the building, like ghosts moving, big and tall.

There was more laughter, and a tearing sound. On the wind, pieces of paper, leaves of books, came whirling among the snow through the dark window. Then a white thing, soaring like a crazy bird, rose up on the wind as if it had wings, and lodged on a black tree outside, struggling. It was the altar-cloth.

There came a bit of gay, trilling music. The wind was running over the organ-pipes like pan-pipes,[3] quickly up and down. Snatches[4] of wild, gay, trilling music, and bursts of the naked low laughter.

'Really!' said the girl. 'This is most extraordinary. Do you hear the music and the people laughing?'

'Yes, I hear somebody on the organ!' said the policeman.

'And do you get the puff of warm wind? Smelling of spring. Almond blossom, that's what it is! A most marvellous scent of almond blossom. *Isn't* it an extraordinary thing!'

She went on triumphantly past the church, and came to the row of little old houses. She entered her own gate in the little railed entrance.

1 blowing in a wild career: the wind rushing wildly.
2 cowed: motionless and depressed by fear.
3 pan-pipes: primitive musical instruments rather like a mouth-organ.
4 snatches: fragments, bits.

'Here I am!' she said finally. 'I'm home now. Thank you very much for coming with me.'

She looked at the young policeman. His whole body was white as a wall with snow, and in the vague light of the arc-lamp from the street his face was humble and frightened.

'Can I come in and warm myself a bit?' he asked humbly. She knew it was fear rather than cold that froze him. He was in mortal fear.

'Well!' she said. 'Stay down in the sitting-room if you like. But don't come upstairs, because I'm alone in the house. You 10 can make up the fire in the sitting-room, and you can go when you are warm.'

She left him on the big, low couch before the fire, his face bluish and blank with fear. He rolled his blue eyes after her as she left the room. But she went up to her bedroom, and fastened her door.

In the morning she was in her studio upstairs in her little house, looking at her own paintings and laughing to herself. Her canaries were talking and shrilly whistling in the sunshine that followed the storm. The cold snow outside was still clean, 20 and the white glare in the air gave the effect of much stronger sunshine than actually existed.

She was looking at her own paintings, and chuckling to herself over their comicalness. Suddenly they struck her as absolutely absurd. She quite enjoyed looking at them, they seemed to her so grotesque. Especially her self-portrait, with its nice brown hair and its slightly opened rabbit-mouth and its baffled, uncertain rabbit eyes. She looked at the painted face and laughed in a long, rippling laugh, till the yellow canaries like faded daffodils almost went mad in an effort to sing louder. The 30 girl's long, rippling laugh sounded through the house uncannily.

The housekeeper, a rather sad-faced young woman of a superior sort—nearly all people in England are of the superior sort, superiority being an English ailment—came in with an inquiring and rather disapproving look.

'Did you call, Miss James?' she asked loudly.

'No. No, I didn't call. Don't shout, I can hear quite well,' replied the girl.

The housekeeper looked at her again. 40

'You knew there was a young man in the sitting-room?' she said.

'No. Really!' cried the girl. 'What, the young policeman? I'd forgotten all about him. He came in in the storm to warm himself. Hasn't he gone?'

'No, Miss James.'

'How extraordinary of him! What time is it? Quarter to nine! Why didn't he go when he was warm? I must go and see him, I suppose.'

'He says he's lame,' said the housekeeper censoriously and loudly.

'Lame! That's extraordinary. He certainly wasn't last night. 10 But don't shout. I can hear quite well.'

'Is Mr Marchbanks coming in to breakfast, Miss James?' said the housekeeper, more and more censorious.

'I couldn't say. But I'll come down as soon as mine is ready. I'll be down in a minute, anyhow, to see the policeman. Extraordinary that he is still here.'

She sat down before her window, in the sun, to think a while. She could see the snow outside, the bare, purplish trees. The air all seemed rare and different. Suddenly the world had become quite different: as if some skin or integument had broken, as if 20 the old, mouldering London sky had crackled and rolled back, like an old skin, shrivelled, leaving an absolutely new blue heaven.

'It really is extraordinary!' she said to herself. 'I certainly saw that man's face. What a wonderful face it was! I shall never forget it. Such laughter! He laughs longest who laughs last. He certainly will have the last laugh. I like him for that: he will laugh last. Must be someone really extraordinary! How very nice to be the one to laugh last. He certainly will. What a wonderful being! I suppose I must call him a being. He's not a 30 person exactly.

'But how wonderful of him to come back and alter all the world immediately! *Isn't* that extraordinary. I wonder if he'll have altered Marchbanks. Of course Marchbanks never *saw* him. But he heard him. Wouldn't that do as well, I wonder!—I *wonder*!'

She went off into a muse about Marchbanks. She and he were *such* friends. They had been friends like that for almost two years. Never lovers. Never that at all. But *friends*.

And after all, she had been in love with him: in her head. 40 This seemed now so funny to her: that she had been, in her head, so much in love with him. After all, life was too absurd.

Because now she saw herself and him as such a funny pair. He so funnily taking life terribly seriously, especially his own life. And she so ridiculously *determined* to save him from himself. Oh, how absurd! *Determined* to save him from himself, and wildly in love with him in the effort. The determination to save him from himself.

Absurd! Absurd! Absurd! Since she had seen the man laughing among the holly-bushes—*such* extraordinary, wonderful laughter—she had seen her own ridiculousness. Really, what fantastic silliness, saving a man from himself! Saving anybody. What fantastic silliness! How much more amusing and lively to let a man go to perdition in his own way. Perdition was more amusing than salvation anyhow, and a much better place for most men to go to.

She had never been in love with any man, and only spuriously in love with Marchbanks. She saw it quite plainly now. After all, what nonsense it all was, this being-in-love business. Thank goodness she had never made the humiliating mistake.

No, the man among the holly-bushes had made her see it all so plainly: the ridiculousness of being in love, the *infra dig.*[1] business of chasing a man or being chased by a man.

'Is love *really* so absurd and *infra dig.*?' she said aloud to herself.

'Why of course!' came a deep, laughing voice.

She stared round, but nobody was to be seen.

'I expect it's that man again!' she said to herself. 'It really *is* remarkable, you know, I consider it's a remarkable thing that I never really wanted a man, *any* man. And there I am over thirty. It *is* curious. Whether it's something wrong with me, or right with me, I can't say. I don't know till I've proved it. But I believe, if that man kept on laughing something would happen to me.'

She smelt the curious smell of almond blossom in the room, and heard the distant laugh again.

'I do wonder why Marchbanks went with that woman last night—the Jewish-looking woman. Whatever could he want of her?—or she of him? So strange, as if they both had made up their minds to something! How extraordinarily puzzling life is! So messy, it all seems.

'Why does nobody ever laugh in life like that man? He *did* seem so wonderful. So scornful! And so proud! And *so* real!

[1] *infra dig.*: below one's dignity.

59

With those laughing, scornful, amazing eyes, just laughing and disappearing again. I can't imagine him chasing a Jewish-looking woman. Or chasing any woman, thank goodness. It's all *so* messy. My policeman would be messy if one would let him: like a dog. I do dislike dogs, really I do. And men do seem so doggy!—'

But even while she mused, she began to laugh again to herself with a long, low chuckle. How wonderful of that man to come and laugh like that and make the sky crack and shrivel like an old skin. Wasn't he wonderful! Wouldn't it be wonderful if he 10 just touched her. Even touched her. She felt, if he touched her, she herself would emerge new and tender out of an old, hard skin. She was gazing abstractedly out of the window.

'There he comes, just now,' she said abruptly. But she meant Marchbanks, not the laughing man.

There he came, his hands still shoved down in his overcoat pockets, his head still rather furtively ducked, in the bowler hat, and his legs still rather shambling.[1] He came hurrying across the road, not looking up, deep in thought, no doubt. Thinking profoundly, with agonies of agitation, no doubt about his last 20 night's experience. It made her laugh.

She, watching from the window above, burst into a long laugh, and the canaries went off their heads again.

He was in the hall below. His resonant voice was calling, rather imperiously:

'James! Are you coming down?'

'No,' she called. 'You come up.'

He came up two at a time, as if his feet were a bit savage with the stairs for obstructing him.

In the doorway he stood staring at her with a vacant, sardonic 30 look, his grey eyes moving with a queer light. And she looked back at him with a curious, rather haughty carelessness.

'Don't you want your breakfast?' she asked. It was his custom to come and take breakfast with her each morning.

'No,' he answered loudly. 'I went to a tea-shop.'

'Don't shout,' she said. 'I can hear you quite well.'

He looked at her with mockery and a touch of malice.

'I believe you always could,' he said, still loudly.

'Well, anyway, I can now, so you needn't shout,' she replied.

And again his grey eyes, with the queer, greyish phospho- 40 rescent gleam in them, lingered malignantly on her face.

[1] shambling: moving in an awkward and irregular way.

'Don't look at me,' she said calmly. 'I know all about everything.'

He burst into a pouf[1] of malicious laughter.

'Who taught you—the policeman?' he cried.

'Oh, by the way, he must be downstairs! No, he was only incidental. So, I suppose, was the woman in the shawl. Did you stay all night?'

'Not entirely. I came away before dawn. What did you do?'

'Don't shout. I came home long before dawn.' And she seemed 10 to hear the long, low laughter.

'Why, what's the matter?' he said curiously. 'What have you been doing?'

'I don't quite know. Why?—are you going to call me to account?'

'Did you hear that laughing?'

'Oh, yes. And many more things. And saw things too.'

'Have you seen the paper?'

'No. Don't shout, I can hear.'

'There's been a great storm, blew out the windows and doors 20 of the church outside here, and pretty well wrecked the place.'

'I saw it. A leaf of the church Bible blew right in my face: from the Book of Job[2]—' She gave a low laugh.

'But what else did you see?' he cried loudly.

'I saw *him*.'

'Who?'

'Ah, that I can't say.'

'But what was he like?'

'That I can't tell you. I don't really know.'

'But you must know. Did your policeman see him too?' 30

'No, I don't suppose he did. My policeman!' And she went off into a long ripple of laughter. 'He is by no means mine. But I *must* go downstairs and see him.'

'It's certainly made you very strange,' Marchbanks said. 'You've got no *soul*, you know.'

'Oh, thank goodness for that!' she cried. 'My policeman has one, I'm sure. *My policeman!*' and she went off again into a long peal of laughter, the canaries pealing shrill accompaniment.

[1] pouf: an onomatopoeic word suggesting the sound of the expulsion of air as he laughs scornfully.

[2] Book of Job: a book of the Bible concerned with the struggle of a deeply religious soul with the doubts aroused by undeserved suffering.

'What's the matter with you?' he said.

'Having no soul. I never had one really. It was always fobbed off on me.[1] Soul was the only thing there was between you and me. Thank goodness it's gone. Haven't you lost yours? The one that seemed to worry you, like a decayed tooth?'

'But what are you *talking* about?' he cried.

'I don't know,' she said. 'It's all so extraordinary. But look here, I *must* go down and see my policeman. He's downstairs in the sitting-room. You'd better come with me.'

They went down together. The policeman, in his waistcoat and shirt-sleeves, was lying on the sofa, with a very long face.

'Look here!' said Miss James to him. 'Is it true you're lame?'

'It is true. That's why I'm here. I can't walk,' said the fair-haired young man as tears came to his eyes.

'But how did it happen? You weren't lame last night,' she said.

'I don't know how it happened—but when I woke up and tried to stand up, I couldn't do it.' The tears ran down his distressed face.

'How very extraordinary!' she said. 'What can we do about it?'

'Which foot is it?' asked Marchbanks. 'Let us have a look at it.'

'I don't like to,' said the poor devil.

'You'd better,' said Miss James.

He slowly pulled off his stocking, and showed his white left foot curiously clubbed,[2] like the weird paw of some animal. When he looked at it himself, he sobbed.

And as he sobbed, the girl heard again the low, exulting laughter. But she paid no heed to it, gazing curiously at the weeping young policeman.

'Does it hurt?' she asked.

'It does if I try to walk on it,' wept the young man.

'I'll tell you what,' she said. 'We'll telephone for a doctor, and he can take you home in a taxi.'

The young fellow shamefacedly wiped his eyes.

'But have you no idea how it happened?' asked Marchbanks anxiously.

'I haven't myself,' said the young fellow.

[1] fobbed off on me: she feels that it is unfairly and wrongly thought that she has a soul.

[2] clubbed: a distortion of the foot normally giving a lumpy appearance.

At that moment the girl heard the low, eternal laugh right in her ear. She started,[1] but could see nothing.

She started round again as Marchbanks gave a strange, yelping cry, like a shot animal. His white face was drawn,[2] distorted in a curious grin, that was chiefly agony but partly wild recognition. He was staring with fixed eyes at something. And in the rolling agony of his eyes was the horrible grin of a man who realizes he has made a final, and this time fatal, fool of himself.

'Why,' he yelped in a high voice, 'I knew it was he!' And with a queer shuddering laugh he pitched[3] forward on the carpet and lay writhing for a moment on the floor. Then he lay still, in a weird, distorted position, like a man struck by lightning.

Miss James stared with round, staring brown eyes.

'Is he dead?' she asked quickly.

The young policeman was trembling so that he could hardly speak. She could hear his teeth chattering.[4]

'Seems like it,' he stammered.

There was a faint smell of almond blossom in the air.

Useful Phrases

1 to take something in (page 47, line 24)—to understand the meaning.
2 to get something (page 47, line 25)—to understand the meaning.
3 to perk up (page 49, line 37)—to become less depressed and more lively.
4 to be wrapped up in something (page 50, line 37)—to be fascinated by or deeply involved in.
5 to slope off (page 51, line 4)—to move away rather secretively and often to avoid work.
6 to make eyes at someone (page 52, line 39)—to look amorously at someone.
7 to have one's tail between one's legs (page 56, line 13)—feeling humiliated or depressed.

[1] started: moved suddenly through fear.
[2] drawn: tense and weary in his expression.
[3] pitched: fell headlong.
[4] chattering: knocking together through fright.

8 to call someone to account (page 61, line 14)—to want to know a person's movements often for the purpose of being angry about what they have done.

9 to have a long face (page 62, line 11)—to look very sad and depressed.

10 to pay heed to something (page 62, line 30)—to take notice of, to pay attention to.

Questions to guide the reader and also for further discussion or essay writing

1 Explain carefully what the author is trying to express in the following quotations:

a 'the sharp, night-bird call of the girl' (page 47, line 31).

b 'She watched him, on tiptoes of alertness' (page 48, lines 2 & 3).

c 'Except that one is always expecting Somebody, you know' (page 52, lines 37 & 38).

d 'The London air was no longer heavy and clammy, saturated with ghosts of the unwilling dead' (page 54, lines 39 & 40).

e 'Then obscured lightning winked through the snow in the air' (page 55, lines 6 & 7).

f 'the canaries went off their heads again' (page 60, line 23).

2 Write a brief character sketch of Miss James.

3 What are the principal physical differences between March-banks and the policeman?

4 Suggest what you feel are the main themes of this story.

5 In what ways does the author use descriptions of Nature to give extra depth to his story?

6 'After all, life was too absurd' (page 58, line 42). How far does the ending of the story tend to suggest this is true?

KATHERINE MANSFIELD

Feuille d'Album*

KATHERINE MANSFIELD was born in
Wellington, New Zealand in 1888, but she
completed her education in England. She
planned a musical career, but married in 1909
and did not fulfil her ambition. She was
divorced from her first husband in 1913 and
in the same year married John Middleton
Murry, the well-known literary critic.

Ill health made it necessary for her to travel
much in France and Germany and in 1911
her first collection of short stories was
published. Her reputation as an individual
and brilliant short-story writer was
established with her second volume—*Bliss*
(1920).

After her early death in 1923 several other
collections of her stories, and a number of
poems, journals, and letters, were edited and
published by her husband.

* The meaning of the title is: a page from an album or scrapbook.

HE REALLY WAS an impossible person. Too shy altogether. With absolutely nothing to say for himself. And such a weight.[1] Once he was in your studio he never knew when to go, but would sit on and on until you nearly screamed, and burned to throw something enormous after him when he did finally blush his way out—something like the tortoise stove.[2] The strange thing was that at first sight he looked most interesting. Everybody agreed about that. You would drift into the café one evening and there you would see, sitting in a corner, with a glass of coffee in front of him, a thin dark boy, wearing a blue jersey 10 with a little grey flannel jacket buttoned over it. And somehow that blue jersey and the grey jacket with the sleeves that were too short gave him the air of a boy that has made up his mind to run away to sea. Who has run away, in fact, and will get up in a moment and sling a knotted handkerchief containing his nightshirt and his mother's picture on the end of a stick, and walk out into the night and be drowned. . . . Stumble over the wharf edge on his way to the ship, even. . . . He had black close-cropped hair, grey eyes with long lashes, white cheeks and a mouth pouting as though he were determined not to cry. . . . How 20 could one resist him? Oh, one's heart was wrung at sight. And, as if that were not enough, there was his trick of blushing. . . . Whenever the waiter came near him he turned crimson—he might have been just out of prison and the waiter in the know. . . .

'Who is he, my dear? Do you know?'

'Yes. His name is Ian French. Painter. Awfully clever, they say. Someone started by giving him a mother's tender care. She asked him how often he heard from home, whether he had enough blankets on his bed, how much milk he drank a day. But when she went round to his studio to give an eye to his socks, 30 she rang and rang, and though she could have sworn she heard someone breathing inside, the door was not answered. . . . Hopeless!'

Someone else decided that he ought to fall in love. She summoned him to her side, called him 'boy', leaned over him so that he might smell the enchanting perfume of her hair, took his arm, told him how marvellous life could be if one only had the courage, and went round to his studio one evening and rang and rang. . . . Hopeless.

[1] a weight: here means a person who is so quiet that he is difficult to spend much time with.

[2] tortoise stove: a very slow burning cooking apparatus.

'What the poor boy really wants is thoroughly rousing,' said a third. So off they went to cafés and cabarets, little dances, places where you drank something that tasted like tinned apricot juice, but cost twenty-seven shillings a bottle and was called champagne, other places, too thrilling for words, where you sat in the most awful gloom, and where someone had always been shot the night before. But he did not turn a hair. Only once he got very drunk, but instead of blossoming forth, there he sat, stony, with two spots of red on his cheeks, like, my dear, yes, the dead image of that rag-time[1] thing they were playing, like a 'Broken Doll'. But when she took him back to his studio he had quite recovered, and said 'good night' to her in the street below, as though they had walked home from church together. . . . Hopeless.

After heaven knows how many more attempts—for the spirit of kindness dies very hard in women—they gave him up. Of course, they were still perfectly charming, and asked him to their shows, and spoke to him in the café but that was all. When one is an artist one has no time simply for people who won't respond. Has one?

'And besides I really think there must be something rather fishy somewhere . . . don't you? It can't all be as innocent as it looks! Why come to Paris if you want to be a daisy in the field? No, I'm not suspicious. But—'

He lived at the top of a tall mournful building overlooking the river. One of those buildings that look so romantic on rainy nights and moonlight nights, when the shutters are shut, and the heavy door, and the sign advertising 'a little apartment to let immediately' gleams forlorn beyond words. One of those buildings that smell so unromantic all the year round, and where the concierge lives in a glass cage on the ground floor, wrapped up in a filthy shawl, stirring something in a saucepan and ladling out tit-bits to the swollen old dog lolling on a bead cushion. . . . Perched up in the air the studio had a wonderful view. The two big windows faced the water; he could see the boats and the barges swinging up and down, and the fringe of an island planted with trees, like a round bouquet. The side window looked across to another house, shabbier still and smaller, and down below there was a flower market. You could see the tops of huge umbrellas, with frills of bright flowers escaping from them, booths

[1] rag-time: music of American negro origin, which was very popular as dance-music in the 1920s.

covered with striped awning where they sold plants in boxes and
clumps of wet gleaming palms in terra-cotta[1] jars. Among the
flowers the old women scuttled from side to side, like crabs.
Really there was no need for him to go out. If he sat at the window until his white beard fell over the sill he still would have
found something to draw. . . .

How surprised those tender women would have been if they
had managed to force the door. For he kept his studio as neat as
a pin. Everything was arranged to form a pattern, a little 'still
life'[2] as it were—the saucepans with their lids on the wall 10
behind the gas stove, the bowl of eggs, milk-jug and teapot on
the shelf, the books and the lamp with the crinkly paper shade
on the table. An Indian curtain that had a fringe of red leopards
marching round it covered his bed by day, and on the wall
beside the bed on a level with your eyes when you were lying
down there was a small neatly printed notice: GET UP AT ONCE.

Every day was much the same. While the light was good he
slaved at his painting, then cooked his meals and tidied up the
place. And in the evenings he went off to the café, or sat at home
reading or making out the most complicated list of expenses 20
headed: 'What I ought to be able to do it on,' and ending with a
sworn statement . . . 'I swear not to exceed this amount for next
month. Signed, Ian French.'

Nothing very fishy about this; but those far-seeing women
were quite right. It wasn't all.

One evening he was sitting at the side window eating some
prunes and throwing the stones on to the tops of the huge
umbrellas in the deserted flower market. It had been raining—
the first real spring rain of the year had fallen—a bright spangle
hung on everything, and the air smelled of buds and moist earth. 30
Many voices sounding languid and content rang out in the dusky
air, and the people who had come to close their windows and
fasten the shutters leaned out instead. Down below in the market
the trees were peppered with new green. What kind of trees
were they? he wondered. And now came the lamplighter. He
stared at the house across the way, the small, shabby house, and
suddenly, as if in answer to his gaze, two wings of windows
opened and a girl came out on to the tiny balcony carrying a
pot of daffodils. She was a strangely thin girl in a dark pinafore,[3]

[1] terra-cotta: a red substance made from a mixture of clay and sand.
[2] 'still-life': a picture representing inanimate objects.
[3] pinafore: a garment worn over clothes to protect them from dirt.

68

with a pink handkerchief tied over her hair. Her sleeves were rolled up almost to her shoulders and her slender arms shone against the dark stuff.

'Yes, it is quite warm enough. It will do them good,' she said, putting down the pot and turning to someone in the room inside. As she turned she put her hands up to the handkerchief and tucked away some wisps of hair. She looked down at the deserted market and up at the sky, but where he sat there might have been a hollow in the air. She simply did not see the house opposite. And then she disappeared. 10

His heart fell out of the side window of his studio, and down to the balcony of the house opposite—buried itself in the pot of daffodils under the half-opened buds and spears of green. . . . That room with the balcony was the sitting-room, and the one next door to it was the kitchen. He heard the clatter of the dishes as she washed up after supper, and then she came to the window, knocked a little mop against the ledge, and hung it on a nail to dry. She never sang or unbraided her hair, or held out her arms to the moon as young girls are supposed to do. And she always wore the same dark pinafore and the pink handkerchief over 20 her hair. . . . Whom did she live with? Nobody else came to those two windows, and yet she was always talking to someone in the room. Her mother, he decided, was an invalid. They took in sewing. The father was dead. . . . He had been a journalist—very pale, with long moustaches, and a piece of black hair falling over his forehead.

By working all day they just made enough money to live on, but they never went out and they had no friends. Now when he sat down at his table he had to make an entirely new set of sworn statements. . . . Not to go to the side window before a 30 certain hour: signed, Ian French. Not to think about her until he had put away his painting things for the day: signed, Ian French.

It was quite simple. She was the only person he really wanted to know, because she was, he decided, the only other person alive who was just his age. He couldn't stand giggling girls, and he had no use for grown-up women. . . . She was his age, she was —well, just like him. He sat in his dusky studio, tired, with one arm hanging over the back of his chair, staring in at her window and seeing himself in there with her. She had a violent temper; they 40 quarrelled terribly at times, he and she. She had a way of stamping her foot and twisting her hands in her pinafore . . . furious.

And she very rarely laughed. Only when she told him about an absurd little kitten she once had who used to roar and pretend to be a lion when it was given meat to eat. Things like that made her laugh. . . . But as a rule they sat together very quietly; he, just as he was sitting now, and she with her hands folded in her lap and her feet tucked under, talking in low tones, or silent and tired after the day's work. Of course, she never asked him about his pictures, and of course he made the most wonderful drawings of her which she hated, because he made her so thin and so dark. . . . But how could he get to know her? This might go on for 10 years. . . .

Then he discovered that once a week, in the evenings, she went out shopping. On two successive Thursdays she came to the window wearing an old-fashioned cape over the pinafore, and carrying a basket. From where he sat he could not see the door of her house, but on the next Thursday evening at the same time he snatched up his cap and ran down the stairs. There was a lovely pink light over everything. He saw it glowing in the river, and the people walking towards him had pink faces and pink hands. 20

He leaned against the side of his house waiting for her and he had no idea of what he was going to do or say. 'Here she comes,' said a voice in his head. She walked very quickly, with small, light steps; with one hand she carried the basket, with the other she kept the cape together. . . . What could he do? He could only follow. . . . First she went into the grocer's and spent a long time in there, and then she went into the butcher's where she had to wait her turn. Then she was an age at the draper's matching something, and then she went to the fruit shop and bought a lemon. As he watched her he knew more surely than 30 ever he must get to know her, now. Her composure, her seriousness and her loneliness, the very way she walked as though she was eager to be done with this world of grown-ups all was so natural to him and so inevitable.

'Yes, she is always like that,' he thought proudly. 'We have nothing to do with these people.'

But now she was on her way home and he was as far off as ever. . . . She suddenly turned into the dairy and he saw her through the window buying an egg. She picked it out of the basket with such care—a brown one, a beautifully shaped one, 40 the one he would have chosen. And when she came out of the dairy he went in after her. In a moment he was out again, and following her past his house across the flower market, dodging among the huge umbrellas and treading on the fallen flowers and the round marks where the pots had stood. . . . Through her door he crept, and up the stairs after, taking care to tread in time with her so that she would not notice. Finally, she stopped on the landing,[1] and took the key out of her purse. As she put it into the door he ran up and faced her.

Blushing more crimson than ever, but looking at her severely he said, almost angrily: 'Excuse me, Mademoiselle, you dropped this.'   10

And he handed her an egg.

Useful Phrases

1 to be in the know (page 66, line 24)—to have knowledge of something (often with a suggestion of sharing secret or restricted information).

2 not to turn a hair (page 67, line 7)—to show no sign of emotion, to be completely unmoved.

3 to blossom forth (page 67, line 8)—to become more talkative and open out as a personality (as a flower opens out in spring-time).

4 something rather fishy (page 67, line 21)—something which is suspicious.

5 not to be able to stand (page 69, line 36)—not to be able to tolerate or put up with.

6 to be an age at (page 70, line 28)—to be a very long time at a place.

Questions to guide the reader and also for further discussion or essay writing

1 Explain carefully what the author is trying to express in the following quotations:

a 'Oh, one's heart was wrung at sight' (page 66, line 21).

b 'the dead image of' (page 67, line 10).

c 'to be a daisy in the field?' (page 67, line 23).

d '—a bright spangle hung on everything,' (page 68, lines 29 & 30).

e 'the trees were peppered with new green' (page 68, line 34).

f 'His heart fell out of the side window of his studio,' (page 69, line 11).

[1] landing: the level part of a staircase between the flights of stairs.

2 Write a character study of Ian French using your own words.

3 What do the largely physical and external descriptions of the girl tell the reader about her probable character and way of life?

4 '—for the spirit of kindness dies very hard in women—' (page 67, lines 15 & 16). Enlarge upon this belief of the author's.

5 'When one is an artist one has no time simply for people who won't respond' (page 67, lines 18–20). What do you think the author means by this? How far do you imagine this to be true?

W. SOMERSET MAUGHAM

The Bum*

W. SOMERSET MAUGHAM—the son of an
English solicitor—was born in Paris in 1874,
and lived there until he was ten. He was
educated at King's School, Canterbury, and
later at Heidelberg University. Subsequently
he studied medicine at St. Thomas's Hospital
in London, but the success of his first novel,
Liza of Lambeth (1897) persuaded him to give
up his medical studies and devote his life to
writing instead.

Just before and immediately after the First
World War he had considerable success as a
playwright, and several of his plays were
received enthusiastically on the London stage.
The last play he wrote was *Sheppey* (1933). He
has also won great acclaim as a novelist, and
as a writer of short stories and travel books.
He travelled in most parts of the world, and
since 1930, lived mostly at Cap Ferrat in the
South of France, where he died in 1966.

For many years he has had a very wide
reading public, and is acknowledged to be one
of the greatest of modern English short-story
writers.

* The title suggests an idle, good-for-nothing tramp.

G OD KNOWS HOW often I had lamented that I had not half the time I needed to do half the things I wanted. I could not remember when last I had had a moment to myself. I had often amused my fancy with the prospect of just one week's complete idleness. Most of us when not busy working are busy playing; we ride, play tennis or golf, swim or gamble; but I saw myself doing nothing at all. I would lounge through the morning, dawdle through the afternoon, and loaf through the evening. My mind would be a slate and each passing hour a sponge that wiped out the scribblings written on it by the world of sense. Time, because it is so fleeting, time, because it is beyond recall, is the most precious of human goods and to squander it is the most delicate form of dissipation in which man can indulge. Cleopatra dissolved in wine a priceless pearl, but she gave it to Antony to drink; when you waste the brief golden hours you take the beaker in which the gem is melted and dash its contents to the ground. The gesture is grand and like all grand gestures absurd. That of course is its excuse. In the week I promised myself I should naturally read, for to the habitual reader reading is a drug of which he is the slave; deprive him of printed matter and he grows nervous, moody, and restless; then, like the alcoholic bereft of brandy who will drink shellac[1] or methylated spirit, he will make do with the advertisements of a paper five years old; he will make do with a telephone directory. But the professional writer is seldom a disinterested reader. I wished my reading to be but another form of idleness. I made up my mind that if ever the happy day arrived when I could enjoy untroubled leisure I would complete an enterprise that had always tempted me, but which hitherto, like an explorer making reconnaissances into an undiscovered country, I had done little more than enter upon: I would read the entire works of Nick Carter.[2]

But I had always fancied myself choosing my moment with surroundings to my liking, not having it forced upon me; and when I was suddenly faced with nothing to do and had to make the best of it (like a steamship acquaintance whom in the wide waste of the Pacific Ocean you have invited to stay with you in London and who turns up without warning and with all his luggage) I was not a little taken aback. I had come to Vera Cruz[3]

[1] shellac: a resin purified from the deposit left on trees in the East by the lac insect.

[2] Nick Carter: an imaginary author.

[3] Vera Cruz: a port on the east coast of Mexico.

from Mexico City to catch one of the Ward Company's
white cool ships to Yucatan;[1] and found to my dismay that, a
dock strike having been declared over-night, my ship would not
put in. I was stuck in Vera Cruz. I took a room in the Hotel
Diligencias overlooking the *plaza*, and spent the morning looking at the sights of the town. I wandered down side streets and
peeped into quaint courts. I sauntered through the parish
church; it is picturesque with its gargoyles and flying buttresses,
and the salt wind and the blazing sun have patined[2] its harsh
and massive walls with the mellowness of age; its cupola is 10
covered with white and blue tiles. Then I found that I had seen
all that was to be seen and I sat down in the coolness of the
arcade that surrounded the square and ordered a drink. The sun
beat down on the *plaza* with a merciless splendour. The coco-
palms drooped dusty and bedraggled. Great black buzzards
perched on them for a moment uneasily, swooped to the ground
to gather some bit of offal, and then with lumbering wings flew
up to the church tower. I watched the people crossing the square;
Negroes, Indians, Creoles, and Spanish, the motley people of the
Spanish Main;[3] and they varied in colour from ebony to ivory. 20
As the morning wore on, the tables around me filled up, chiefly
with men, who had come to have a drink before luncheon, for
the most part in white ducks,[4] but some notwithstanding the heat
in the dark clothes of professional respectability. A small band,
a guitarist, a blind fiddler, and a harpist, played rag-time[5] and
after every other tune the guitarist came round with a plate. I
had already bought the local paper and I was adamant to the
newsvendors who pertinaciously sought to sell me more copies
of the same sheet. I refused, oh, twenty times at least, the
solicitations of grimy urchins who wanted to shine my spotless 30
shoes; and having come to the end of my small change I could
only shake my head at the beggars who importuned me. They
gave one no peace. Little Indian women, in shapeless rags, each
one with a baby tied in the shawl on her back, held out skinny
hands and in a whimper recited a dismal screed; blind men were
led up to my table by small boys; the maimed, the halt, the
deformed exhibited the sores and the monstrosities with which

[1] Yucatan: a region in the south-east of Mexico.
[2] patined: made shiny and polished looking.
[3] Spanish Main: Caribbean Sea.
[4] white ducks: trousers made of white sailcloth material.
[5] rag-time: music of American negro origin.

75

nature or accident had afflicted them; and half naked, underfed children whined endlessly their demand for coppers. But these kept their eyes open for the fat policeman who would suddenly dart out on them with a thong and give them a sharp cut on the back or over the head. Then they would scamper, only to return again when, exhausted by the exercise of so much energy, he relapsed into lethargy.

But suddenly my attention was attracted by a beggar who, unlike the rest of them and indeed the people sitting round me, swarthy and black-haired, had hair and beard of a red so vivid 10 that it was startling. His beard was ragged and his long mop of hair looked as though it had not been brushed for months. He wore only a pair of trousers and a cotton singlet, but they were tatters, grimy and foul, that barely held together. I have never seen anyone so thin; his legs, his naked arms were but skin and bone, and through the rents of his singlet you saw every rib of his wasted body; you could count the bones of his dust-covered feet. Of that starveling band he was easily the most abject. He was not old, he could not well have been more than forty, and I could not but ask myself what had brought him to this pass. It was absurd to 20 think that he would not have worked if work he had been able to get. He was the only one of the beggars who did not speak. The rest of them poured forth their litany of woe and if it did not bring the alms they asked continued until an impatient word from you chased them away. He said nothing. I suppose he felt that his look of destitution was all the appeal he needed. He did not even hold out his hand, he merely looked at you, but with such wretchedness in his eyes, such despair in his attitude, it was dreadful; he stood on and on, silent and immobile, gazing stead-fastly, and then, if you took no notice of him, he moved slowly 30 to the next table. If he was given nothing he showed neither disappointment nor anger. If someone offered him a coin he stepped forward a little, stretched out his claw-like hand, took it without a word of thanks, and impassively went his way. I had nothing to give him and when he came to me, so that he should not wait in vain, I shook my head.

' "*Dispense Usted por Dios*",[1] I said, using the polite Castillian formula with which the Spaniards refuse a beggar.

But he paid no attention to what I said. He stood in front of me, for as long as he stood at the other tables, looking at me with 40 tragic eyes. I have never seen such a wreck of humanity. There

[1] 'Dispense Usted por Dios': literally means—For God's sake forgive me.

was something terrifying in his appearance. He did not look quite sane. At length he passed on.

It was one o'clock and I had lunch. When I awoke from my siesta it was still very hot, but towards evening a breath of air coming in through the windows which I had at last ventured to open tempted me into the *plaza*. I sat down under my arcade and ordered a long drink. Presently people in greater numbers filtered into the open space from the surrounding streets, the tables in the restaurants round it filled up, and in the kiosk in the middle the band began to play. The crowd grew thicker. 10 On the free benches people sat huddled together like dark grapes clustered on a stalk. There was a lively hum of conversation. The big black buzzards flew screeching overhead, swooping down when they saw something to pick up, or scurrying away from under the feet of the passers-by. As twilight descended they swarmed, it seemed from all parts of the town, towards the church tower; they circled heavily about it and hoarsely crying, squabbling, and jangling, settled themselves uneasily to roost. And again bootblacks begged me to have my shoes cleaned, newsboys pressed dank papers upon me, beggars whined their plaintive 20 demand for alms. I saw once more that strange, red-bearded fellow and watched him stand motionless, with the crushed and piteous air, before one table after another. He did not stop before mine. I supposed he remembered me from the morning and having failed to get anything from me then thought it useless to try again. You do not often see a red-haired Mexican, and because it was only in Russia that I had seen men of so destitute a mien I asked myself if he was by chance a Russian. It accorded well enough with the Russian fecklessness that he should have allowed himself to sink to such a depth of degradation. Yet he had 30 not a Russian face; his emaciated features were clear-cut, and his blue eyes were not set in the head in a Russian manner; I wondered if he could be a sailor, English, Scandinavian, or American, who had deserted his ship and by degrees sunk to this pitiful condition. He disappeared. Since there was nothing else to do, I stayed on till I got hungry, and when I had eaten came back. I sat on till the thinning crowd suggested it was bed-time. I confess that the day had seemed long and I wondered how many similar days I should be forced to spend there.

But I woke after a little while and could not get to sleep again. 40 My room was stifling. I opened the shutters and looked out at the church. There was no moon, but the bright stars faintly lit its outline. The buzzards were closely packed on the cross above the cupola and on the edges of the tower, and now and then they moved a little. The effect was uncanny. And then, I have no notion why, that red scarecrow recurred to my mind and I had suddenly a strange feeling that I had seen him before. It was so vivid that it drove away from me the possibility of sleep. I felt sure that I had come across him, but when and where I could not tell. I tried to picture the surroundings in which he might take his place, but I could see no more than a dim figure against a background of fog. As the dawn approached it grew a little 10 cooler and I was able to sleep.

I spent my second day at Vera Cruz as I had spent the first. But I watched for the coming of the red-haired beggar, and as he stood at the tables near mine I examined him with attention. I felt certain now that I had seen him somewhere. I even felt certain that I had known him and talked to him, but I still could recall none of the circumstances. Once more he passed my table without stopping and when his eyes met mine I looked in them for some gleam of recollection. Nothing. I wondered if I had made a mistake and thought I had seen him in the same way as 20 sometimes, by some queer motion of the brain, in the act of doing something you are convinced that you are repeating an action that you have done at some past time. I could not get out of my head the impression that at some moment he had entered into my life. I racked my brains. I was sure now that he was either English or American. But I was shy of addressing him. I went over in my mind the possible occasions when I might have met him. Not to be able to place him exasperated me as it does when you try to remember a name that is on the tip of your tongue and yet eludes you. The day wore on. 30

Another day came, another morning, another evening. It was Sunday and the *plaza* was more crowded than ever. The tables under the arcade were packed. As usual the red-haired beggar came along, a terrifying figure in his silence, his threadbare rags, and his pitiful distress. He was standing in front of a table only two from mine, mutely beseeching, but without a gesture. Then I saw the policeman who at intervals tried to protect the public from the importunities of all these beggars sneak round a column and give him a resounding whack with his thong. His thin body winced, but he made no protest and showed no resentment; he 40 seemed to accept the stinging blow as in the ordinary course of things, and with his slow movements slunk away into the gathering night of the *plaza*. But the cruel stripe had whipped my memory and suddenly I remembered.

Not his name, that escaped me still, but everything else. He must have recognized me, for I have not changed very much in twenty years, and that was why after that first morning he had never paused in front of my table. Yes, it was twenty years since I had known him. I was spending a winter in Rome and every evening I used to dine in a restaurant in the Via Sistina where you got excellent macaroni and a good bottle of wine. It was frequented by a little band of English and American art students, 10 and one or two writers; and we used to stay late into the night engaged in interminable arguments upon art and literature. He used to come in with a young painter who was a friend of his. He was only a boy then, he could not have been more than twenty-two; and with his blue eyes, straight nose, and red hair he was pleasing to look at. I remembered that he spoke a great deal of Central America, he had had a job with the American Fruit Company, but had thrown it over because he wanted to be a writer. He was not popular among us because he was arrogant and we were none of us old enough to take the arrogance of youth 20 with tolerance. He thought us poor fish and did not hesitate to tell us so. He would not show us his work, because our praise meant nothing to him and he despised our censure. His vanity was enormous. It irritated us; but some of us were uneasily aware that it might perhaps be justified. Was it possible that the intense consciousness of genius that he had, rested on no grounds? He had sacrificed everything to be a writer. He was so certain of himself that he infected some of his friends with his own assurance.

I recalled his high spirits, his vitality, his confidence in the 30 future, and his disinterestedness. It was impossible that it was the same man, and yet I was sure of it. I stood up, paid for my drink, and went out into the *plaza* to find him. My thoughts were in a turmoil. I was aghast. I had thought of him now and then and idly wondered what had become of him. I could never have imagined that he was reduced to this frightful misery. There are hundreds, thousands of youths who enter upon the hard calling of the arts with extravagant hopes; but for the most part they come to terms with their mediocrity and find somewhere in life a niche where they can escape starvation. This was awful. I asked 40 myself what had happened. What hopes deferred had broken his spirit, what disappointments shattered him, and what lost illusions ground him to the dust? I asked myself if nothing could be done. I walked round the *plaza*. He was not in the arcades. There was no hope of finding him in the crowd that circled round the band-stand. The light was waning and I was afraid I had lost him. Then I passed the church and saw him sitting on the steps. I cannot describe what a lamentable object he looked. Life had taken him, rent him on its racks,[1] torn him limb from limb, and then flung him, a bleeding wreck, on the stone steps of that church. I went up to him.

'Do you remember Rome?' I said.   10

He did not move. He did not answer. He took no more notice of me than if I were not standing before him. He did not look at me. His vacant blue eyes rested on the buzzards that were screaming and tearing at some object at the bottom of the steps. I did not know what to do. I took a yellow-backed note out of my pocket and pressed it in his hand. He did not give it a glance. But his hand moved a little, the thin claw-like fingers closed on the note and scrunched it up; he made it into a little ball and then edging it on to his thumb flicked it into the air so that it fell among the jangling buzzards. I turned my head instinctively and saw one of 20 them seize it in his beak and fly off followed by two others screaming behind it. When I looked back the man was gone.

I stayed three more days in Vera Cruz. I never saw him again.

Useful Phrases

1 to fancy oneself (page 74, line 32)—to imagine oneself doing something (can also mean to have a high opinion of oneself).
2 to be taken aback (page 74, line 38)—to be greatly surprised or shocked.
3 to rack one's brains (page 78, line 25)—to search in one's mind for the required information.
4 to place someone (page 78, line 28)—to know who someone is and in what circumstances one met them.
5 to throw something over (page 79, line 18)—to abandon or give something up.
6 to be aghast (page 79, line 34)—to be horrified or stupefied.
7 to come to terms with (page 79, line 39)—to accept or submit to circumstances.

[1] racks: instruments of torture on which the victim is stretched.

Questions to guide the reader and also for further discussion or essay writing

1   Explain carefully what the author is trying to express in the
    following quotations:
 a 'I would lounge through the morning, dawdle through the after-
    noon, and loaf through the evening' (page 74, lines 7 & 8).
 b 'On the free benches people sat huddled together like dark grapes
    clustered on a stalk' (page 77, lines 11 & 12).
 c 'newsboys pressed dank papers upon me,' (page 77, lines 19 & 20).
 d 'but I could see no more than a dim figure against a background
    of fog' (page 78, lines 9 & 10).
 e 'But the cruel stripe had whipped my memory' (page 79, line 1).
 f 'He thought us poor fish' (page 79, line 21).

2   What attitude does this story suggest towards artists? To what
    extent would you agree with this?

3   What does the ending of the story imply and how does it fit in
    with the rest of the story?

4   'Most of us when not busy working are busy playing;' (page 74,
    line 5). How true is this of modern life? What does the
    author say constitutes complete relaxation? Would you agree
    with his opinion?

5   'Time, because it is so fleeting, time, because it is beyond recall,
    is the most precious of human goods and to squander it is the
    most delicate form of dissipation in which man can indulge'
    (page 79, lines 10–13). How far do you agree with the sentiment
    expressed here?

6   'the arrogance of youth' (page 79, line 20). Could this be said to
    be the theme of the story? Use this quotation as the topic for an
    essay or discussion.

SAKI

Sredni Vashtar

'SAKI' whose real name was H. H. Munro,
was born in Burma in 1870, of a family with
strong Anglo-Indian military connexions. His
childhood was spent largely in England,
where he attended Bedford Grammar School.
After spending some time with his father on
the continent, he went to Burma to join the
Military Police in 1893.

Some time after he had been invalided
home, he decided to earn his living by
writing in London. His first book *The Rise of
the Russian Empire* was completed in 1899, and
from then on he travelled widely in Europe as
a journalist, and also became known as a
short story writer.

In 1908 he returned to England and
established his reputation as a very successful
writer of tragi-comic stories. In 1914 he joined
the Army and went to France where he fought
until he was killed in November 1916.

CONRADIN WAS TEN years old, and the doctor had pronounced his professional opinion that the boy would not live another five years. The doctor was silky and effete, and counted for little, but his opinion was endorsed by Mrs De Ropp, who counted for nearly everything. Mrs De Ropp was Conradin's cousin and guardian, and in his eyes she represented those three-fifths of the world that are necessary and disagreeable and real; the other two-fifths, in perpetual antagonism to the foregoing, were summed up in himself and his imagination. One of these days Conradin supposed he would succumb to the mastering pressure of wearisome necessary things—such as illnesses and coddling restrictions and drawn-out dullness. Without his imagination, which was rampant under the spur of loneliness, he would have succumbed long ago.

Mrs De Ropp would never, in her honestest moments, have confessed to herself that she disliked Conradin, though she might have been dimly aware that thwarting him 'for his good' was a duty which she did not find particularly irksome. Conradin hated her with a desperate sincerity which he was perfectly able to mask. Such few pleasures as he could contrive for himself gained an added relish from the likelihood that they would be displeasing to his guardian, and from the realm of his imagination she was locked out—an unclean thing, which should find no entrance.

In the dull, cheerless garden, overlooked by so many windows that were ready to open with a message not to do this or that, or a reminder that medicines were due, he found little attraction. The few fruit-trees that it contained were set jealously apart from his plucking, as though they were rare specimens of their kind blooming in an arid waste; it would probably have been difficult to find a market-gardener who would have offered ten shillings for their entire yearly produce. In a forgotten corner, however, almost hidden behind a dismal shrubbery, was a disused toolshed of respectable proportions, and within its walls Conradin found a haven, something that took on the varying aspects of a play-room and a cathedral. He had peopled it with a legion of familiar phantoms, evoked partly from fragments of history and partly from his own brain, but it also boasted two inmates of flesh and blood. In one corner lived a ragged-plumaged Houdan hen,[1] on which the boy lavished an affection that had scarcely another outlet. Further back in the gloom stood a large hutch, divided into two compartments, one of which was fronted with

[1] Houdan hen: a type of large-crested fowl of Turkish origin.

close iron bars. This was the abode of a large polecat-ferret[1]
which a friendly butcher-boy had once smuggled, cage and all,
into its present quarters, in exchange for a long-secreted hoard of
small silver. Conradin was dreadfully afraid of the lithe, sharp-
fanged beast, but it was his most treasured possession. Its very
presence in the tool-shed was a secret and fearful joy, to be kept
scrupulously from the knowledge of the Woman, as he privately
dubbed his cousin. And one day, out of Heaven knows what
material, he spun the beast a wonderful name, and from that
moment it grew into a god and a religion. The Woman indulged 10
in religion once a week at a church near by, and took Conradin
with her, but to him the church service was an alien rite in the
House of Rimmon.[2] Every Thursday, in the dim and musty
silence of the toolshed, he worshipped with mystic and elaborate
ceremonial before the wooden hutch where dwelt Sredni Vashtar,
the great ferret. Red flowers in their season and scarlet berries in
the winter-time were offered at his shrine, for he was a god who
laid some special stress on the fierce impatient side of things, as
opposed to the Woman's religion, which, as far as Conradin
could observe, went to great lengths in the contrary direction. 20
And on great festivals powdered nutmeg[3] was strewn in front of
his hutch, an important feature of the offering being that the
nutmeg had to be stolen. These festivals were of irregular occur-
rence, and were chiefly appointed to celebrate some passing event.
On one occasion, when Mrs De Ropp suffered from acute toothache for three days, Conradin kept up the festival during the
entire three days, and almost succeeded in persuading himself
that Sredni Vashtar was personally responsible for the toothache.
If the malady had lasted for another day the supply of nutmeg
would have given out.   30
    The Houdan hen was never drawn into the cult of Sredni
Vashtar. Conradin had long ago settled that she was an Anabaptist.[4] He did not pretend to have the remotest knowledge as
to what an Anabaptist was, but he privately hoped that it was
dashing and not very respectable. Mrs De Ropp was the ground
plan on which he based and detested all respectability.

    [1] polecat-ferret: a cross between a large weasel and a small animal used to
catch rabbits.
    [2] The House of Rimmon: the temple of Babylon mentioned in the Bible.
    [3] nutmeg: a spice made from the nuts of an East Indian tree.
    [4] Anabaptist: a person who believes that baptism should only be ad-
ministered to adults.

After a while Conradin's absorption in the tool-shed began to attract the notice of his guardian. 'It is not good for him to be pottering down there in all weathers,' she promptly decided, and at breakfast one morning she announced that the Houdan hen had been sold and taken away overnight. With her short-sighted eyes she peered at Conradin, waiting for an outbreak of rage and sorrow, which she was ready to rebuke with a flow of excellent precepts and reasoning. But Conradin said nothing: there was nothing to be said. Something perhaps in his white set face gave her a momentary qualm, for at tea that afternoon there was 10 toast on the table, a delicacy which she usually banned on the ground that it was bad for him; also because the making of it 'gave trouble', a deadly offence in the middle-class feminine eye.

'I thought you liked toast,' she exclaimed, with an injured air, observing that he did not touch it.

'Sometimes,' said Conradin.

In the shed that evening there was an innovation in the worship of the hutch-god. Conradin had been wont to chant his praises, tonight he asked a boon.[1]   20

'Do one thing for me, Sredni Vashtar.'

The thing was not specified. As Sredni Vashtar was a god he must be supposed to know. And choking back a sob as he looked at that other empty corner, Conradin went back to the world he so hated.

And every night, in the welcome darkness of his bedroom, and every evening in the dusk of the tool-shed, Conradin's bitter litany[2] went up: 'Do one thing for me, Sredni Vashtar.'

Mrs De Ropp noticed that the visits to the shed did not cease, and one day she made a further journey of inspection.   30

'What are you keeping in that locked hutch?' she asked. 'I believe it's guinea-pigs. I'll have them all cleared away.'

Conradin shut his lips tight, but the Woman ransacked his bedroom till she found the carefully hidden key, and forthwith marched down to the shed to complete her discovery. It was a cold afternoon, and Conradin had been bidden to keep to the house. From the furthest window of the dining-room the door of the shed could just be seen beyond the corner of the shrubbery, and there Conradin stationed himself. He saw the Woman enter, and then he imagined her opening the door of the sacred hutch 40

[1] a boon: a favour or special request.
[2] litany: a form of prayer used in public worship.

85

and peering down with her shortsighted eyes into the thick
straw bed where his god lay hidden. Perhaps she would prod at
the straw in her clumsy impatience. And Conradin fervently
breathed his prayer for the last time. But he knew as he prayed
that he did not believe. He knew that the Woman would come
out presently with that pursed smile he loathed so well on her
face, and that in an hour or two the gardener would carry away
his wonderful god, a god no longer, but a simple brown ferret in
a hutch. And he knew that the Woman would triumph always
as she triumphed now, and that he would grow ever more sickly 10
under her pestering and domineering and superior wisdom, till
one day nothing would matter much more with him, and the
doctor would be proved right. And in the sting and misery of his
defeat, he began to chant loudly and defiantly the hymn of his
threatened idol:

> 'Sredni Vashtar went forth,
> His thoughts were red thoughts and his teeth were white.
> His enemies called for peace, but he brought them death.
> Sredni Vashtar the Beautiful.'

And then of a sudden he stopped his chanting and drew closer 20
to the window-pane. The door of the shed still stood ajar as it had
been left, and the minutes were slipping by. They were long
minutes, but they slipped by nevertheless. He watched the
starlings[1] running and flying in little parties across the lawn;
he counted them over and over again, with one eye always on
that swinging door. A sour-faced maid came in to lay the table
for tea, and still Conradin stood and waited and watched. Hope
had crept by inches into his heart, and now a look of triumph began to blaze in his eyes that had only known the wistful patience of
defeat. Under his breath, with a furtive exultation, he began once 30
again the pæan[2] of victory and devastation. And presently his
eyes were rewarded: out through that doorway came a long, low,
yellow-and-brown beast, with eyes a-blink at the waning daylight, and dark wet stains around the fur of jaws and throat.
Conradin dropped on his knees. The great polecat-ferret made
its way down to a small brook at the foot of the garden, drank
for a moment, then crossed a little plank bridge and was lost to
sight in the bushes. Such was the passing of Sredni Vashtar.

[1] starlings: small black birds with brown spots.
[2] pæan: a song of triumph.

'Tea is ready,' said the sour-faced maid; 'where is the mistress?'

'She went down to the shed some time ago,' said Conradin.

And while the maid went to summon her mistress to tea, Conradin fished a toasting-fork out of the sideboard drawer and proceeded to toast himself a piece of bread. And during the toasting of it and the buttering of it with much butter and the slow enjoyment of eating it, Conradin listened to the noises and silences which fell in quick spasms beyond the dining-room door. The loud foolish screaming of the maid, the answering chorus of 10 wondering ejaculations from the kitchen region, the scuttering footsteps and hurried embassies for outside help, and then, after a lull,[1] the scared sobbings and the shuffling tread of those who bore a heavy burden into the house.

'Whoever will break it to the poor child? I couldn't for the life of me!' exclaimed a shrill voice. And while they debated the matter among themselves, Conradin made himself another piece of toast.

Useful Phrases

1 to dub someone (page 84, line 8)—to give someone a nickname.
2 to lay stress on (page 84, line 18)—to put emphasis on or to attach particular importance to.
3 to be dashing (page 84, line 35)—full of life, rather exotic.
4 to be wont to do (page 85, line 19)—to be accustomed to, to do something habitually.
5 to be ajar (page 86, line 21)—to be partially open.
6 'I couldn't for the life of me!' (page 87, lines 15 & 16)—I couldn't under any possible circumstances.

Questions to guide the reader and also for further discussion or essay writing

1 Explain carefully what the author is trying to express in the following quotations:
a 'The doctor was silky and effete,' (page 83, line 3).
b 'his imagination, which was rampant under the spur of loneliness,' (page 83, lines 13 & 14).
c 'He had peopled it with a legion of familiar phantoms,' (page 83, lines 35 & 36).

[1] a lull: an interval of calm.

d 'the making of it "gave trouble", a deadly offence in the middle-class feminine eye' (page 85, lines 12 & 13).

e 'the welcome darkness of his bedroom,' (page 85, line 26).

f 'with eyes a-blink at the waning daylight,' (page 86, lines 33 & 34).

2 What are the significant differences between the separate 'religions' of Conradin and Mrs. de Ropp? What do they tell you about their different characters?

3 What is Conradin's reaction to the polecat ferret? In what ways is it (*a*) similar (*b*) different to his reaction to his guardian?

4 Write a brief character sketch of Conradin.

5 'Mrs. de Ropp was the ground plan on which he based and detested all respectability' (page 84, lines 35 & 36). To what extent do you feel this quotation to be the central theme of the story?

6 Explain the significance of the words in the final paragraph of the story—'Whoever will break it to the poor child?'—in the context of the whole story.

EVELYN WAUGH

Tactical Exercise

EVELYN WAUGH, the son of a publisher and
literary critic, was born in London in 1903.
After being educated at Lancing School, and
Hertford College, Oxford, he studied art in
London and then spent a short time teaching
in a private school.

In 1928 his first novel—*Decline and Fall*—was
published, and in 1930 he became a Roman
Catholic. During the 1930s he travelled
widely and wrote several books based on his
various experiences.

He became a war-correspondent in 1935,
and served as an officer during the Second
World War. From 1937 until his death in
1966, he and his family lived in
Gloucestershire.

He is best known for his novels of social
satire and entertainment. These, with his
travel books and short stories, have made him
one of the most famous of contemporary
English writers.

JOHN VERNEY MARRIED Elizabeth in 1938, but it was not until the winter of 1945 that he came to hate her steadily and fiercely. There had been countless brief gusts of hate before this, for it was a thing which came easily to him. He was not what is normally described as a bad-tempered man, rather the reverse; a look of fatigue and abstraction was the only visible sign of the passion which possessed him, as others are possessed by laughter or desire, several times a day.

During the war he passed among those he served with as a phlegmatic fellow. He did not have his good or his bad days; 10 they were all uniformly good or bad; good in that he did what had to be done, expeditiously without ever 'getting in a flap' or 'going off the deep end'; bad from the intermittent, invisible sheet-lightning of hate which flashed and flickered deep inside him at every obstruction or reverse. In his orderly room[1] when, as a company commander, he faced the morning procession of defaulters and malingerers; in the mess[2] when the subalterns[3] disturbed his reading by playing the wireless; at the Staff College when the 'syndicate' disagreed with his solution; at Brigade H.Q. when the staff-sergeant mislaid a file or the 20 telephone orderly muddled a call; when the driver of his car missed a turning; later, in hospital, when the doctor seemed to look cursorily at his wound and the nurses stood gossiping jauntily at the beds of more likeable patients instead of doing their duty to him—in all the annoyances of army life which others dismissed with an oath and a shrug, John Verney's eyelids dropped wearily, a tiny grenade of hate exploded, and the fragments rang and ricocheted round the steel walls of his mind.

There had been less to annoy him before the war. He had some money and the hope of a career in politics. Before marriage 30 he served his apprenticeship to the Liberal party in two hopeless by-elections.[4] The Central Office then rewarded him with a constituency[5] in outer London which offered a fair chance in the next general election. In the eighteen months before the war he nursed this constituency from his flat in Belgravia[6] and travelled

[1] orderly room: the administrative centre of an army unit.
[2] the mess: the place where officers eat and relax.
[3] subalterns: army officers below the rank of captain.
[4] by-elections: elections during a Parliamentary session to fill a vacant position.
[5] a constituency: a community represented by a Member of Parliament.
[6] Belgravia: the smart and very expensive residential area of London.

frequently on the Continent to study political conditions. These studies convinced him that war was inevitable; he denounced the Munich agreement[1] pungently and secured a commission in the Territorial Army.[2]

Into the peacetime life Elizabeth fitted unobtrusively. She was his cousin. In 1938 she had reached the age of twenty-six, four years his junior, without falling in love. She was a calm, handsome young woman, an only child, with some money of her own and more to come. As a girl, in her first season,[3] an injudicious remark, let slip and overheard, got her the reputation of clever- 10 ness. Those who knew her best ruthlessly called her 'deep'.

Thus condemned to social failure, she languished in the ballrooms of Pont Street[4] for another year and then settled down to a life of concert-going and shopping with her mother, until she surprised her small circle of friends by marrying John Verney. Courtship and consummation were tepid, cousinly, harmonious. They agreed, in face of coming war, to remain childless. No one knew what Elizabeth felt or thought about anything. Her judgements were mainly negative, deep or dull as you cared to take them. She had none of the appearance of a woman likely to in- 20 flame great hate.

John Verney was discharged from the Army early in 1945 with a M.C.[5] and one leg, for the future, two inches shorter than the other. He found Elizabeth living in Hampstead with her parents, his uncle and aunt. She had kept him informed of the changes in her condition, but, preoccupied, he had not clearly imagined them. Their flat had been requisitioned by a government office; their furniture and books sent to a repository and totally lost, partly burned by a bomb, partly pillaged by firemen. Elizabeth, who was a linguist, had gone to work in a clandestine branch of 30 the Foreign Office.

Her parents' house had once been a substantial Georgian villa overlooking the Heath.[6] John Verney arrived there early in the

[1] The Munich agreement: the 1938 settlement between England and Germany that delayed the outbreak of war.

[2] a commission in the Territorial Army: an appointment as an officer in the British Reserve Army.

[3] first season: the year in which debutantes are introduced into Society.

[4] Pont Street: a street in London associated with wealthy, upper middle-class Society.

[5] a M.C.: Military Cross; a decoration.

[6] the Heath: Hampstead Heath; the open parkland in a London suburb.

morning after a crowded night's journey from Liverpool.[1] The wrought-iron railings and gates had been rudely torn away by the salvage collectors, and in the front garden, once so neat, weeds and shrubs grew in a rank jungle trampled at night by courting soldiers. The back garden was a single, small bomb-crater; heaped clay, statuary, and the bricks and glass of ruined greenhouses; dry stalks of willow-herb stood breast high over the mounds. All the windows were gone from the back of the house, replaced by shutters of card and board, which put the main rooms in perpetual darkness. 'Welcome to Chaos and Old Night,'[2] said his uncle genially.

There were no servants; the old had fled, the young had been conscribed for service. Elizabeth made him some tea before leaving for her office.

Here he lived, lucky, Elizabeth told him, to have a home. Furniture was unprocurable, furnished flats commanded a price beyond their income, which was now taxed to a bare wage. They might have found something in the country, but Elizabeth, being childless, could not get release from her work. Moreover, he had his constituency.

This, too, was transformed. A factory wired round like a prisoner-of-war camp stood in the public gardens. The streets surrounding it, once the trim houses of potential Liberals, had been bombed, patched, confiscated, and filled with an immigrant proletarian population. Every day he received a heap of complaining letters from constituents exiled in provincial boarding-houses. He had hoped that his decoration and his limp might earn him sympathy, but he found the new inhabitants indifferent to the fortunes of war. Instead they showed a sceptical curiosity about Social Security. 'They're nothing but a lot of reds,'[3] said the Liberal agent.

'You mean I shan't get in?'

'Well, we'll give them a good fight. The Tories[4] are putting up a Battle-of-Britain pilot. I'm afraid he'll get most of what's left of the middle-class vote.'

In the event John Verney came bottom of the poll, badly. A rancorous Jewish school-teacher was elected. The Central Office

[1] Liverpool: a large port in the north of England.

[2] 'Welcome to Chaos and Old Night,': a reference to the words in Milton's *Paradise Lost* (Book I—line 540).

[3] reds: Communists.

[4] The Tories: the familiar name for the Conservative Party.

paid his deposit, but the election had cost him dear. And when it was over there was absolutely nothing for John Verney to do.

He remained in Hampstead, helped his aunt make the beds after Elizabeth had gone to her office, limped to the green-grocer and fishmonger, and stood, full of hate, in the queues; helped Elizabeth wash up at night. They ate in the kitchen, where his aunt cooked deliciously the scanty rations.[1] His uncle went three days a week to help pack parcels for Java.

Elizabeth, the deep one, never spoke of her work, which, in fact, was concerned with setting up hostile and oppressive govern-ments in Eastern Europe. One evening at a restaurant, a man came and spoke to her, a tall young man whose sallow aquiline face was full of intellect and humour. 'That's the head of my department,' she said. 'He's so amusing.'

'Looks like a Jew.'

'I believe he is. He's a strong Conservative and hates the work,' she added hastily, for since his defeat in the election John had become fiercely anti-Semitic.[2]

'There is absolutely no need to work for the State now,' he said. 'The war's over.'

'Our work is just beginning. They won't let any of us go. You must understand what conditions are in this country.'

It often fell to Elizabeth to explain 'conditions' to him. Strand by strand, knot by knot, through the coalless winter, she exposed the vast net of governmental control which had been woven in his absence. He had been reared in traditional Liberalism and the system revolted him. More than this, it had him caught, personally, tripped up, tied, tangled; wherever he wanted to go, whatever he wanted to do or have done, he found himself baffled and frustrated. And as Elizabeth explained she found herself defending. This regulation was necessary to avoid that ill; such a country was suffering, as Britain was not, for having neglected such a precaution; and so on, calmly and reasonably.

'I know it's maddening, John, but you must realize it's the same for everyone.'

'That's what all you bureaucrats want,' he said. 'Equality through slavery. The two-class state—proletarians and officials.'

---

[1] rations: the restricted amount of food allowed to people during war-time.

[2] anti-Semitic: against Jewish peoples.

Elizabeth was part and parcel of it. She worked for the State and the Jews. She was a collaborator with the new, alien, occupying power. And as the winter wore on and the gas burned feebly in the stove, and the rain blew in through the patched windows, as at length spring came and buds broke in the obscene wilderness round the house, Elizabeth in his mind became something more important. She became a symbol. For just as soldiers in far-distant camps think of their wives, with a tenderness they seldom felt at home, as the embodiment of all the good things they have left behind, wives who perhaps were scolds and drabs, but in the desert and jungle become transfigured until their trite air-letters become texts of hope, so Elizabeth grew in John Verney's despairing mind to more than human malevolence as the archpriestess and maenad[1] of the century of the common man.

'You aren't looking well, John,' said his aunt. 'You and Elizabeth ought to get away for a bit. She is due for leave at Easter.'

'The State is granting her a supplementary ration of her husband's company, you mean. Are we sure she has filled in all the correct forms? Or are commissars of her rank above such things?'

Uncle and aunt laughed uneasily. John made his little jokes with such an air of weariness, with such a droop of the eyelids that they sometimes struck chill in that family circle. Elizabeth regarded him gravely and silently.

John was far from well. His leg was in constant pain so that he no longer stood in queues. He slept badly; as also, for the first time in her life, did Elizabeth. They shared a room now, for the winter rains had brought down ceilings in many parts of the shaken house and the upper rooms were thought to be unsafe. They had twin beds on the ground floor in what had once been her father's library.

In the first days of his homecoming John had been amorous. Now he never approached her. They lay night after night six feet apart in the darkness. Once when John had been awake for two hours he turned on the lamp that stood on the table between them. Elizabeth was lying with her eyes wide open staring at the ceiling.

'I'm sorry. Did I wake you?'

[1] maenad: a woman almost mad with excitement—(originally a female follower of Bacchus, the God of wine, in Greek mythology).

'I haven't been asleep.'

'I thought I'd read for a bit. Will it disturb you?'

'Not at all.'

She turned away. John read for an hour. He did not know whether she was awake or asleep when he turned off the light.

Often after that he longed to put on the light, but was afraid to find her awake and staring. Instead, he lay, as others lie in a luxurious rapture of love, hating her.

It did not occur to him to leave her; or, rather, it did occur 10 from time to time, but he hopelessly dismissed the thought. Her life was bound tight to his; her family was his family; their finances were intertangled and their expectations lay together in the same quarters. To leave her would be to start fresh, alone and naked in a strange world; and lame and weary at the age of thirty-eight, John Verney had not the heart to move.

He loved no one else. He had nowhere to go, nothing to do. Moreover he suspected, of late, that it would not hurt her if he went. And, above all, the single steadfast desire left to him was to do her ill. 'I wish she were dead,' he said to himself as he lay 20 awake at night. 'I wish she were dead.'

Sometimes they went out together. As the winter passed, John took to dining once or twice a week at his club. He assumed that on these occasions she stayed at home, but one morning it transpired that she too had dined out the evening before. He did not ask with whom, but his aunt did, and Elizabeth replied, 'Just someone from the office.'

'The Jew?' John asked.

'As a matter of fact, it was.'

'I hope you enjoyed it.'   30

'Quite. A beastly dinner, of course, but he's very amusing.'

One night when he returned from his club, after a dismal little dinner and two crowded Tube[1] journeys, he found Elizabeth in bed and deeply asleep. She did not stir when he entered. Unlike her normal habit, she was snoring. He stood for a minute, fascinated by this new and unlovely aspect of her, her head thrown back, her mouth open and slightly dribbling at the corner. Then he shook her. She muttered something, turned over, and slept heavily and soundlessly.

Half an hour later, as he was striving to compose himself for 40 sleep, she began to snore again. He turned on the light, and

[1] Tube: the underground railway trains in London.

95

looked at her more closely and noticed with surprise, which suddenly changed to joyous hope, that there was a tube of unfamiliar pills, half empty, beside her on the bed table.

He examined it. '*24 Comprimés narcotiques, hypnotiques,*'[1] he read, and then in large scarlet letters, 'NE PAS DÉPASSER DEUX.'[2] He counted those which were left. Eleven.

With tremulous butterfly wings hope began to flutter in his heart, became a certainty. He felt a fire kindle and spread inside him until he was deliciously suffused in every limb and organ. He lay, listening to the snores, with the pure excitement of a child on Christmas Eve. 'I shall wake up tomorrow and find her dead,' he told himself, as once he had felt the flaccid stocking[3] at the foot of his bed and told himself, 'Tomorrow I shall wake up and find it full.' Like a child, he longed to sleep to hasten the morning and, like a child, he was wildly ecstatically sleepless. Presently he swallowed two of the pills himself and almost at once was unconscious.

Elizabeth always rose first to make breakfast for the family. She was at the dressing-table when sharply, without drowsiness, his memory stereoscopically clear about the incidents of the night before, John awoke. 'You've been snoring.' she said.

Disappointment was so intense that at first he could not speak. Then he said, 'You snored, too, last night.'

'It must be the sleeping-tablet I took. I must say it gave me a good night.'

'Only one?'

'Yes, two's the most that's safe.'

'Where did you get them?'

'A friend at the office—the one you called the Jew. He has them prescribed by a doctor for when he's working too hard. I told him I wasn't sleeping, so he gave me half a bottle.'

'Could he get me some?'

'I expect so. He can do most things like that.'

So he and Elizabeth began to drug themselves regularly and passed long, vacuous nights. But often John delayed, letting the beatific pill lie beside his glass of water, while knowing the vigil

---

[1] '24 Comprimés narcotiques, hypnotiques,': means that the tube contained 24 sleeping pills.

[2] 'NE PAS DÉPASSER DEUX.': means, do not take more than two.

[3] stocking: here refers to the English custom of hanging up a stocking for presents on the night before Christmas—Christmas Eve.

was terminable at will, he postponed the joy of unconsciousness, heard Elizabeth's snores, and hated her sumptuously.

One evening while the plans for the holiday were still under discussion, John and Elizabeth went to the cinema. The film was a murder story of no great ingenuity but with showy scenery. A bride murdered her husband by throwing him out of a window, down a cliff. Things were made easy for her by his taking a lonely lighthouse for their honeymoon. He was very rich and she wanted his money. All she had to do was to confide in the local doctor and a few neighbours that her husband frightened her by walking 10 in his sleep; she doped his coffee, dragged him from the bed to the balcony—a feat of some strength—where she had already broken away a yard of balustrade, and rolled him over. Then she went back to bed, gave the alarm the next morning, and wept over the mangled body which was presently discovered half awash on the rocks. Retribution overtook her later, but at the time the thing was a complete success.

'I wish it were as easy as that,' thought John, and in a few hours the whole tale had floated away in those lightless attics of the mind where films and dreams and funny stories lie spider- 20 shrouded for a lifetime unless, as sometimes happens, an intruder brings them to light.

Such a thing happened a few weeks later when John and Elizabeth went for their holiday. Elizabeth found the place.

It belonged to someone in her office. It was named Good Hope Fort, and stood on the Cornish[1] coast. 'It's only just been derequisitioned,'[2] she said; 'I expect we shall find it in pretty bad condition.'

'We're used to that,' said John. It did not occur to him that she should spend her leave anywhere but with him. She was as 30 much a part of him as his maimed and aching leg.

They arrived on a gusty April afternoon after a train journey of normal discomfort. A taxi drove them eight miles from the station, through deep Cornish lanes, past granite cottages and disused, archaic tin-workings.[3] They reached the village which gave the houses its postal address, passed through it and out along a track which suddenly emerged from its high banks into

[1] Cornish: the adjective from the word Cornwall—a county in the south-west of England.

[2] derequisitioned: no longer required for military purposes.

[3] archaic tin-workings: places where tin used to be mined, but which are now out of date.

97

open grazing land on the cliff's edge, high, swift clouds and sea-birds wheeling overhead, the turf at their feet alive with flutter-ing wild flowers, salt in the air, below them the roar of the Atlantic breaking on the rocks, a middle-distance of indigo and white tumbled waters and beyond it the serene arc of the horizon. Here was the house.

'Your father,' said John, 'would now say, "Your castle hath a pleasant seat".'[1]

'Well, it has rather, hasn't it?'

It was a small stone building on the very edge of the cliff, built a century or so ago for defensive purposes, converted to a private house in the years of peace, taken again by the Navy during the war as a signal station, now once more reverting to gentler uses. Some coils of rusty wire, a mast, the concrete foundations of a hut, gave evidence of its former masters.

They carried their things into the house and paid the taxi.

'A woman comes up every morning from the village. I said we shouldn't want her this evening. I see she's left us some oil for the lamps. She's got a fire going too, bless her, and plenty of wood. Oh, and look what I've got as a present from father. I promised not to tell you until we arrived. A bottle of whisky. Wasn't it sweet of him. He's been hoarding his ration for three months. . . .' Elizabeth talked brightly as she began to arrange the luggage. 'There's a room for each of us. This is the only proper living-room, but there's a study in case you feel like doing any work. I believe we shall be quite comfortable. . . .'

The living-room was built with two stout bays, each with a French window opening on a balcony which over-hung the sea. John opened one and the sea-wind filled the room. He stepped out, breathed deeply, and then said suddenly: 'Hullo, this is dangerous.'

At one place, between the windows, the cast-iron balustrade had broken away and the stone ledge lay open over the cliff. He looked at the gap and at the foaming rocks below, mo-mentarily puzzled. The irregular polyhedron of memory rolled uncertainly and came to rest.

He had been here before, a few weeks ago, on the gallery of the lighthouse in that swiftly forgotten film. He stood there looking down. It was exactly thus that the waves had come swirling over the rocks, had broken and dropped back with the spray falling

[1] 'Your castle hath a pleasant seat': a quotation from Shakespeare's *Macbeth*.

about them. This was the sound they had made; this was the broken ironwork and the sheer edge.

Elizabeth was still talking in the room, her voice drowned by wind and sea. John returned to the room, shut and fastened the door. In the quiet she was saying '. . . only got the furniture out of store last week. He left the woman from the village to arrange it. She's got some queer ideas, I must say. Just look where she put . . .'

'What did you say this house was called?'

'Good Hope.'   10

'A good name.'

That evening John drank a glass of his father-in-law's whisky, smoked a pipe, and planned. He had been a good tactician. He made a leisurely, mental 'appreciation of the situation'. Object: murder.

When they rose to go to bed he asked: 'You packed the tablets?'

'Yes, a new tube. But I am sure I shan't want any to-night.'

'Neither shall I,' said John, 'the air is wonderful.'   20

During the following days he considered the tactical problem. It was entirely simple. He had the 'staff-solution'[1] already. He considered it in the words and form he had used in the Army. '. . . Courses open to the enemy . . . achievement of surprise . . . consolidation of success.' The staff-solution was exemplary. At the beginning of the first week, he began to put it into execution.

Already, by easy stages, he had made himself known in the village. Elizabeth was a friend of the owner; he the returned hero, still a little strange in civvy street.[2] 'The first holiday my 30 wife and I have had together for six years,' he told them in the golf club and, growing more confidential at the bar, hinted that they were thinking of making up for lost time and starting a family.

On another evening he spoke of war-strain, of how in this war the civilians had had a worse time of it than the services. His wife, for instance; stuck it all through the blitz;[3] office work all

[1] 'staff-solution': the 'official' answer to a problem set by the instructors at the Army Staff College.

[2] civvy street: ordinary, non-military life.

[3] the blitz: the heavy bombardment from the air that London suffered during the Second World War.

day, bombs at night. She ought to get right away, alone somewhere for a long stretch; her nerves had suffered; nothing
serious, but to tell the truth he wasn't quite happy about it. As a
matter of fact he had found her walking in her sleep once or twice
in London.

His companions knew of similar cases; nothing to worry about,
but it wanted watching; didn't want it to develop into anything
worse. Had she seen a doctor?

Not yet, John said. In fact she didn't know she had been sleep-
walking. He had got her back to bed without waking her. He   10
hoped the sea air would do her good. In fact, she seemed
much better already. If she showed any more signs of the
trouble when they got home, he knew a very good man to take
her to.

The golf club was full of sympathy. John asked if there were a
good doctor in the neighbourhood. Yes, they said, old Mackenzie
in the village, a first-class man wasted in a little place like this;
not at all stick-in-the-mud.[1] Read the latest books, psychology
and all that. They couldn't think why Old Mack had never
specialized and made a name for himself.   20

'I think I might go and talk to Old Mack about it,' said
John.

'Do. You couldn't find a better fellow.'

Elizabeth had a fortnight's leave. There were still three days
to go when John went off to the village to consult Dr Mackenzie.
He found a grey-haired, genial bachelor in a consulting room
that was more like a lawyer's office than a physician's, book-
lined, dark, permeated by tobacco smoke.

Seated in the shabby leather armchair he developed in more
precise language the story he had told in the golf club. Dr   30
Mackenzie listened without comment.

'It's the first time I've run against anything like this,' he
concluded.

At length Dr Mackenzie said: 'You got pretty badly knocked
about in the war, Mr Verney?'

'My knee. It still gives me trouble.'

'Bad time in hospital?'

'Three months. A beastly place outside Rome.'

'There's always a good deal of nervous shock in an injury of
that kind. It often persists when the wound is healed.'   40

[1] stick-in-the-mud: a person who is very unprogressive, and reluctant to
keep up with modern developments.

'Yes, but I don't quite understand. . . .'

'My dear Mr Verney, your wife asked me to say nothing about it, but I think I must tell you that she has already been here to consult me on this matter.'

'About her sleep-walking? But she can't. . . .' Then John stopped.

'My dear fellow, I quite understand. She thought you didn't know. Twice lately you've been out of bed and she had to lead you back. She knows all about it.'

John could find nothing to say.   10

'It's not the first time,' Dr Mackenzie continued, 'that I've been consulted by patients who have told me their symptoms and said they had come on behalf of friends or relations. Usually it's girls who think they're in a family way.[1] It's an interesting feature of your case that you should want to ascribe the trouble to someone else, probably the decisive feature. I've given your wife the name of a man in London who I think will be able to help you. Meanwhile I can advise plenty of exercise, light meals at night. . . .'

John Verney limped back to Good Hope Fort in a state of 20 consternation. Security had been compromised; the operation must be cancelled; initiative had been lost . . . all the phrases of the tactical school came to his mind, but he was still numb after this unexpected reverse. A vast and naked horror peeped at him and was thrust aside.

When he got back Elizabeth was laying the supper table. He stood on the balcony and stared at the gaping rails with eyes smarting with disappointment. It was dead calm that evening. The rising tide lapped and fell and mounted again silently among the rocks below. He stood gazing down, then he turned back 30 into the room.

There was one large drink left in the whisky bottle. He poured it out and swallowed it. Elizabeth brought in the supper and they sat down. Gradually his mind grew a little calmer. They usually ate in silence. At last he said: 'Elizabeth, why did you tell the doctor I had been walking in my sleep?'

She quietly put down the plate she had been holding and looked at him curiously. 'Why?' she said gently. 'Because I was worried, of course. I didn't think you knew about it.'

'But have I been?'   40

'Oh yes, several times—in London and here. I didn't think

[1] in a family way: expecting a child, pregnant.

it mattered at first, but the night before last I found you on the balcony, quite near that dreadful hole in the rails. I was really frightened. But it's going to be all right now. Dr Mackenzie has given me the name . . .'

It was possible, thought John Verney; nothing was more likely.

He had lived night and day for ten days thinking of that opening, of the sea and rock below, the ragged ironwork and the sharp edge of stone. He suddenly felt defeated, sick and stupid, as he had as he lay on the Italian hillside with his smashed knee. Then as now he had felt weariness even more than pain.

'Coffee, darling.'

Suddenly he roused himself. 'No,' he almost shouted. 'No, no, no.'

'Darling, what is the matter? Don't get excited. Are you feeling ill? Lie down on the sofa near the window.'

He did as he was told. He felt so weary that he could barely move from his chair.

'Do you think coffee would keep you awake, love? You look quite fit to drop already. There, lie down.'

He lay down, like the tide slowly mounting among the rocks below, sleep rose and spread in his mind. He nodded and woke with a start.

'Shall I open the window, darling, and give you some air?'

'Elizabeth,' he said, 'I feel as if I have been drugged.' Like the rocks below the window—now awash, now emerging clear from falling water; now awash again deeper; now barely visible, mere patches on the face of gentle eddying foam—his brain was softly drowning. He roused himself, as children do in nightmare, still scared, still half asleep. 'I can't be drugged,' he said loudly, 'I never touched the coffee.'

'Drugs in the coffee?' said Elizabeth gently, like a nurse soothing a fractious child. 'Drugs in the "*coffee*"? What an absurd idea. That's the kind of thing that only happens on the films, darling.'

He did not hear her. He was fast asleep, snoring stertorously by the open window.

Useful Phrases

1 'getting in a flap' (page 90, line 12)—becoming very excited or worked up.
2 'going off the deep end' (page 90, line 13)—expressing strong feelings—especially anger—forcefully.
3 to fall to someone (page 93, line 24)—to be their task.
4 to be part and parcel of (page 94, line 1)—to be an essential part.
5 not to have the heart to do something (page 95, line 16)—to be dispirited and lack the courage to do something.
6 to bring something to light (page 97, line 22)—to reveal something hidden or forgotten.
7 to stick something (page 99, line 37)—to endure something.
8 to run against (page 100, line 32)—to encounter or come into contact with.
9 dead calm (page 101, line 28)—absolutely calm, no movement on the sea.
10 'fit to drop' (page 102, line 21)—extremely exhausted physically.

Questions to guide the reader and also for further discussion or essay writing

1 Explain carefully what the author is trying to express in the following quotations:
a 'the intermittent, invisible sheet-lightning of hate' (page 90, lines 13 & 14).
b 'Those who knew her best ruthlessly called her "deep"' (page 91, line 11).
c 'Courtship and consummation were tepid, cousinly, harmonious' (page 91, line 16).
d 'With tremulous butterfly wings hope began to flutter in his heart,' (page 96, lines 7 & 8).
e 'A vast and naked horror peeped at him and was thrust aside' (page 101, lines 24 & 25).

2 How did the war affect (a) John Verney, (b) his wife and (c) their relationship? How far do you sympathize with John Verney on account of his war experiences, and particularly because of the wound he received?

3 Why didn't John Verney leave Elizabeth?

4 Explain the irony of the end of the story.

103

5 'The State is granting her a supplementary ration of her husband's company, you mean. . . .' (page 94, lines 19 & 20). Why does John Verney say this? Is it the State or his wife that he really despises?

6 ' "That's what all you bureaucrats want," he said, "Equality through slavery. The two-class state—proletarians and officials" ' (page 93, lines 37 & 38). What does John Verney mean by this? How far do you think this is true of contemporary life?

VIRGINIA WOOLF

Kew Gardens*

VIRGINIA WOOLF was born in London in
1882. She was educated at home by her father
—Sir Leslie Stephen—and in 1912 married
Leonard Woolf. She and her husband
established the now famous Hogarth Press in
1917.

She began to publish her fiction at the
beginning of the First World War, and
belonged to a group of writers called 'The
Bloomsbury Group'. She was largely
concerned with enlarging the previously
restricted subject matter thought suitable for
fiction at the beginning of this century in
England. Often her works are a combination
of primarily autobiographical material and a
method of poetic intensity, and this is seen
most successfully in her novel *To The
Lighthouse* (1927) which is generally
acknowledged to be her masterpiece.

At the time of her death in 1941 she had
achieved a prominent place in English fiction
and had also established a very considerable
reputation as a literary critic, essayist, and
writer of short stories.

* Kew Gardens: well-known botanical gardens situated just outside the
centre of London.

F ROM THE OVAL-SHAPED flower-bed there rose perhaps a
hundred stalks spreading into heart-shaped or tongue-shaped
leaves half-way up and unfurling at the tip red or blue or yellow
petals marked with spots of colour raised upon the surface; and
from the red, blue or yellow gloom of the throat emerged a
straight bar, rough with gold dust and slightly clubbed at the
end. The petals were voluminous enough to be stirred by the summer breeze, and when they moved, the red, blue and yellow
lights passed one over the other, staining an inch of the brown
earth beneath with a spot of the moist intricate colour. The light
fell either upon the smooth, grey back of a pebble, or, the shell
of a snail with its brown, circular veins, or falling into a raindrop,
it expanded with such intensity of red, blue and yellow the thin
walls of water that one expected them to burst and disappear.
Instead, the drop was left in a second silver grey once more, and
the light now settled upon the flesh of a leaf, revealing the
branching thread of fibre beneath the surface, and again it
moved on and spread its illumination in the vast green spaces
beneath the dome of the heart-shaped and tongue-shaped leaves.
Then the breeze stirred rather more briskly overhead and the
colour was flashed into the air above, into the eyes of the men and
women who walk in Kew Gardens in July.

The figures of these men and women straggled past the
flower-bed with a curiously irregular movement not unlike that
of the white and blue butterflies who crossed the turf in zig-zag
flights from bed to bed. The man was about six inches in front
of the woman, strolling carelessly, while she bore on with
greater purpose, only turning her head now and then to see that
the children were not too far behind. The man kept this distance
in front of the woman purposely, though perhaps unconsciously,
for he wished to go on with his thoughts.

'Fifteen years ago I came here with Lily,' he thought. 'We sat
somewhere over there by a lake and I begged her to marry me all
through the hot afternoon. How the dragonfly kept circling round
us: how clearly I see the dragonfly and her shoe with the square
silver buckle at the toe. All the time I spoke I saw her shoe and
when it moved impatiently I knew without looking up what she
was going to say: the whole of her seemed to be in her shoe. And
my love, my desire, were in the dragonfly; for some reason I

thought that if it settled there, on that leaf, the broad one with
the red flower in the middle of it, if the dragonfly settled on the
leaf she would say "Yes" at once. But the dragonfly went round
and round: it never settled anywhere—of course not, happily
not, or I shouldn't be walking here with Eleanor and the children. Tell me, Eleanor. D'you ever think of the past?'

'Why do you ask, Simon?'

'Because I've been thinking of the past. I've been thinking of
Lily, the woman I might have married. . . . Well, why are you
silent? Do you mind my thinking of the past?'   10

'Why should I mind, Simon? Doesn't one always think of the
past, in a garden with men and women lying under the trees?
Aren't they one's past, all that remains of it, those men and
women, those ghosts lying under the trees, . . . one's happiness,
one's reality?'

'For me, a square silver shoe buckle and a dragonfly——'

'For me, a kiss. Imagine six little girls sitting before their easels
twenty years ago, down by the side of a lake, painting the water-
lilies, the first red water-lilies I'd ever seen. And suddenly a kiss,
there on the back of my neck. And my hand shook all the after-   20
noon so that I couldn't paint. I took out my watch and marked
the hour when I would allow myself to think of the kiss for five
minutes only—it was so precious—the kiss of an old grey-haired
woman with a wart on her nose, the mother of all my kisses all
my life. Come, Caroline, come, Hubert.'

They walked on past the flower-bed, now walking four abreast,
and soon diminished in size among the trees and looked half
transparent as the sunlight and shade swam over their backs in
large trembling irregular patches.

In the oval flower-bed the snail, whose shell had been stained   30
red, blue and yellow for the space of two minutes or so, now appeared to be moving very slightly in its shell, and next began to
labour over the crumbs of loose earth which broke away and
rolled down as it passed over them. It appeared to have a
definite goal in front of it, differing in this respect from the
singular high stepping angular green insect who attempted to
cross in front of it, and waited for a second with its antennae
trembling as if in deliberation, and then stepped off as rapidly
and strangely in the opposite direction. Brown cliffs with deep
green lakes in the hollows, flat, blade-like trees that waved from   40
root to tip, round boulders of grey stone, vast crumpled surfaces
of a thin crackling texture—all these objects lay across the snail's

progress between one stalk and another to his goal. Before he had decided whether to circumvent the arched tent of a dead leaf or to breast it there came past the bed the feet of other human beings.

This time they were both men. The younger of the two wore an expression of perhaps unnatural calm; he raised his eyes and fixed them very steadily in front of him while his companion spoke, and directly his companion had done speaking he looked on the ground again and sometimes opened his lips only after a long pause and sometimes did not open them at all. The elder 10 man had a curiously uneven and shaky method of walking, jerking his hand forward and throwing up his head abruptly, rather in the manner of an impatient carriage horse tired of waiting outside a house; but in the man these gestures were irresolute and pointless. He talked almost incessantly; he smiled to himself and again began to talk, as if the smile had been an answer. He was talking about spirits—the spirits of the dead, who, according to him, were even now telling him all sorts of odd things about their experiences in Heaven.

'Heaven was known to the ancients as Thessaly, William, and 20 now, with this war, the spirit matter is rolling between the hills like thunder.' He paused, seemed to listen, smiled, jerked his head and continued:

'You have a small electric battery and a piece of rubber to insulate the wire—isolate?—insulate?—well, we'll skip the details, no good going into details that wouldn't be understood— and in short the little machine stands in any convenient position by the head of the bed, we will say, on a neat mahogany stand. All arrangements being properly fixed by workmen under my direction, the widow applies her ear and summons the spirit by 30 sign as agreed. Women! Widows! Women in black——'

Here he seemed to have caught sight of a woman's dress in the distance, which in the shade looked a purple black. He took off his hat, placed his hand upon his heart, and hurried towards her muttering and gesticulating feverishly. But William caught him by the sleeve and touched a flower with the tip of his walk-ing-stick in order to divert the old man's attention. After looking at it for a moment in some confusion the old man bent his ear to it and seemed to answer a voice speaking from it, for he began talking about the forests of Uruguay which he had visited hun- 40 dreds of years ago in company with the most beautiful young woman in Europe. He could be heard murmuring about forests of Uruguay blanketed with the wax petals of tropical roses, nightingales, sea beaches, mermaids, and women drowned at sea, as he suffered himself to be moved on by William, upon whose face the look of stoical patience grew slowly deeper and deeper.

Following his steps so closely as to be slightly puzzled by his gestures came two elderly women of the lower middle class, one stout and ponderous, the other rosy cheeked and nimble. Like most people of their station[1] they were frankly fascinated by any signs of eccentricity betokening a disordered brain, especially in the well-to-do; but they were too far off to be certain whether the gestures were merely eccentric or genuinely mad. After they had scrutinized the old man's back in silence for a moment and given each other a queer, sly look, they went on energetically piecing together their very complicated dialogue:

'Nell, Bert, Lot, Cess, Phil, Pa, he says, I says, she says, I says, I says——'

'My Bert, Sis, Bill, Grandad, the old man, sugar,
    Sugar, flour, kippers, greens,[2]
    Sugar, sugar, sugar.'

The ponderous woman looked through the pattern of falling words at the flowers standing cool, firm, and upright in the earth, with a curious expression. She saw them as a sleeper waking from a heavy sleep sees a brass candlestick reflecting the light in an unfamiliar way, and closes his eyes and opens them, and seeing the brass candlestick again, finally starts broad awake and stares at the candlestick with all his powers. So the heavy woman came to a standstill opposite the oval-shaped flower-bed, and ceased even to pretend to listen to what the other woman was saying. She stood there letting the words fall over her, swaying the top part of her body slowly backwards and forwards, looking at the flowers. Then she suggested that they should find a seat and have their tea.

The snail had now considered every possible method of reaching his goal without going round the dead leaf or climbing over it. Let alone the effort needed for climbing a leaf, he was doubtful whether the thin texture which vibrated with such an alarming crackle when touched even by the tip of his horns would bear his weight; and this determined him finally to creep beneath it, for

---

[1] their station: their position or status in life.
[2] greens: the colloquial name for any green vegetables.

there was a point where the leaf curved high enough from the ground to admit him. He had just inserted his head in the opening and was taking stock of the high brown roof and was getting used to the cool brown light when two other people came past outside on the turf. This time they were both young, a young man and a young woman. They were both in the prime of youth, or even in that season which precedes the prime of youth, the season before the smooth pink folds of the flower have burst their gummy case, when the wings of the butterfly, though fully grown, are motionless in the sun.   10

'Lucky it isn't Friday,' he observed.

'Why? D'you believe in luck?'

'They make you pay sixpence on Friday.'

'What's sixpence anyway? Isn't it worth sixpence?'

'What's "it"—what do you mean by "it"?'

'O, anything—I mean—you know what I mean.'

Long pauses came between each of these remarks; they were uttered in toneless and monotonous voices. The couple stood still on the edge of the flower-bed, and together pressed the end of her parasol deep down into the soft earth. The action and the fact 20 that his hand rested on the top of hers expressed their feelings in a strange way, as these short insignificant words also expressed something, words with short wings for their heavy body of meaning, inadequate to carry them far and thus alighting awkwardly upon the very common objects that surrounded them, and were to their inexperienced touch so massive; but who knows (so they thought as they pressed the parasol into the earth) what precipices aren't concealed in them, or what slopes of ice don't shine in the sun on the other side? Who knows? Who has ever seen this before? Even when she wondered what sort of 30 tea they gave you at Kew, he felt that something loomed up behind her words, and stood vast and solid behind them; and the mist very slowly rose and uncovered—O, Heavens, what were those shapes?—little white tables, and waitresses who looked first at her and then at him; and there was a bill that he would pay with a real two shilling piece, and it was real, all real, he assured himself, fingering the coin in his pocket, real to everyone except to him and to her; even to him it began to seem real; and then—but it was too exciting to stand and think any longer, and he pulled the parasol out of the earth with a jerk 40 and was impatient to find the place where one had tea with other people, like other people.

'Come along, Trissie; it's time we had our tea.'

'Wherever "*does*" one have one's tea?' she asked with the oddest thrill of excitement in her voice, looking vaguely round and letting herself be drawn on down the grass path, trailing her parasol, turning her head this way and that way forgetting her tea, wishing to go down there and then down there, remembering orchids and cranes among wild flowers, a Chinese pagoda and a crimson crested bird; but he bore her on.

Thus one couple after another with much the same irregular and aimless movement passed the flower-bed and were enveloped 10 in layer after layer of green blue vapour, in which at first their bodies had substance and a dash of colour,[1] but later both substance and colour dissolved in the green-blue atmosphere. How hot it was! So hot that even the thrush chose to hop, like a mechanical bird, in the shadow of the flowers, with long pauses between one movement and the next; instead of rambling vaguely the white butterflies danced one above another, making with their white shifting flakes the outline of a shattered marble column above the tallest flowers; the glass roofs of the palmhouse shone as if a whole market full of shiny green umbrellas 20 had opened in the sun; and in the drone of the aeroplane the voice of the summer sky murmured its fierce soul. Yellow and black, pink and snow white, shapes of all these colours, men, women, and children were spotted for a second upon the horizon, and then, seeing the breadth of yellow that lay upon the grass, they wavered and sought shade beneath the trees, dissolving like drops of water in the yellow and green atmosphere, staining it faintly with red and blue. It seemed as if all gross and heavy bodies had sunk down in the heat motionless and lay huddled upon the ground, but their voices went wavering from them as 30 if they were flames lolling from the thick waxen bodies of candles. Voices. Yes, voices. Wordless voices, breaking the silence suddenly with such depth of contentment, such passion of desire, or, in the voices of children, such freshness of surprise; breaking the silence? But there was no silence; all the time the motor omnibuses were turning their wheels and changing their gear; like a vast nest of Chinese boxes all of wrought steel turning ceaselessly one within another the city murmured; on the top of which the voices cried aloud and the petals of myriads of flowers flashed their colours into the air.   40

[1] a dash of colour: a very small amount of colour.

Useful Phrases

1 to walk abreast (page 107, line 26)—to walk side by side.
2 to skip something (page 108, line 25)—to leave something out, to omit.
3 to catch sight of (page 108, line 32)—to notice or to glimpse.
4 to suffer oneself (page 109, line 3)—to allow oneself.
5 well-to-do (page 109, line 11)—rich, prosperous.
6 to start broad awake (page 109, lines 26 & 27)—to become suddenly and completely awake.
7 to come to a standstill (page 109, line 28)—to come to a complete stop.
8 let alone (page 109, line 36)—not to mention, apart from.
9 to take stock of (page 110, line 3)—to examine carefully in order to find out what is there.

Questions to guide the reader and also for further discussion or essay writing

1 Explain carefully what the author is trying to express in the following quotations:
a 'the whole of her seemed to be in her shoe' (page 106, line 38).
b 'shade swam over their backs in large trembling irregular patches' (page 107, lines 28 & 29).
c 'forests of Uruguay blanketed with the wax petals of tropical roses,' (page 108–9, lines 42 & 1).
d 'the season before the smooth pink folds of the flower have burst their gummy case, when the wings of the butterfly, though fully grown, are motionless in the sun' (page 110, lines 7–10).
e 'and in the drone of the aeroplane the voice of the summer sky murmured its fierce soul' (page 111, lines 21 & 22).

2 What differences are suggested between the four groups of people walking in Kew Gardens?

3 What are the descriptions of (a) Nature, (b) machines intended to suggest in the story?

4 Do the various people, or Nature herself, play the more important role in suggesting the main theme of this story?

5 What evidence is there in this story of the writer's poetic sensibility?

6 'Doesn't one always think of the past, . . .?' (page 107, line 11).
What would your reply be to this question?

7 'in the voices of children, such freshness of surprise;' (page 111,
lines 33 & 34). What does the author mean by this? Use this
quotation as the theme for an essay or discussion.

SELECT BIBLIOGRAPHY

This bibliography is intended as a general guide to help the reader select other books by the authors whose stories appear in this volume. I have also included a number of relevant books of a critical or biographical nature.

Wherever possible I have given the paperback editions on account of their greater availability and relative inexpensiveness.

* denotes that the book was not available as a paperback at the time of writing.

ELIZABETH BOWEN

NOVELS
Death of the Heart Penguin Books, *Friends and Relations* Cape,* *House in Paris* Sphere, *The Heat of the Day* Penguin Books, *The Hotel* Cape,* *The Last September* Cape,* *To the North* Cape.*

ESSAYS AND SHORT STORIES
A Day in the Dark and Other Stories Cape,* *Afterthought: Pieces About Writing* Longmans,* *Encounters* Sidgwick & Jackson,* *Look at all those Roses* Cape,* *The Demon Lover* Penguin Books.

FOR FURTHER READING
Bowen's Court (a history of her family) by Elizabeth Bowen Longmans,* Jocelyn Brooke: in the Series *Writers and Their Work* Longmans.

JOSEPH CONRAD

NOVELS
Lord Jim Penguin Books or Everyman Paperbacks, *Nostromo* Penguin Books, *The Nigger of the Narcissus, Typhoon and The Shadow Line* Everyman Paperbacks, *The Secret Agent* Penguin Books or Everyman Paperbacks, *Under Western Eyes* Penguin Books or Everyman Paperbacks, *Victory* Penguin Books, *A Personal Record* (Autobiographical) J. M. Dent.*

ESSAYS AND SHORT STORIES
A Set of Six J. M. Dent,* *Heart of Darkness* contained in '*Youth*'—Corgi Paperbacks, *Tales of Hearsay and Last Essays* J. M. Dent,* *Tales of Unrest* Ernest Benn,* *Twixt Land and Sea* J. M. Dent.*

FOR FURTHER READING
J. Baines: *Joseph Conrad* (*A Critical Biography*) Weidenfeld & Nicolson,* M. C. Bradbrook: *England's Polish Genius* Cambridge University Press,* A. J. Guerard: *Conrad the Novelist* Oxford University Press,* F. R. Leavis: in *The Great Tradition* Penguin Books, Edited: Zdzislaw Najder and translated by Halina Carroll: *Conrad's Polish Background* Oxford University Press * (Letters to and from Polish friends).

E. M. FORSTER

NOVELS

A Passage to India Penguin Books, *A Room With a View* Penguin Books, *Howards End* Penguin Books, *The Longest Journey* Penguin Books, *Where Angels Fear to Tread* Penguin Books, *Maurice* Edward Arnold.*

ESSAYS AND SHORT STORIES

Abinger Harvest Penguin Books *Aspects of the Novel* Penguin Books, *Collected Short Stories* Penguin Books, *The Hill of Devi* Penguin Books, *Two Cheers for Democracy* Penguin Books.

FOR FURTHER READING

F. R. Leavis: in *The Common Pursuit* Penguin Books, Lionel Trilling: *E. M. Forster* Hogarth Press,* J. K. Johnstone: in *The Bloomsbury Group* Secker & Warburg.*

GRAHAM GREENE

NOVELS

A Burnt-out Case Penguin Books, *Brighton Rock* Penguin Books, *Our Man in Havana* Penguin Books, *The Comedians* Penguin Books, *The Confidential Agent* Penguin Books, *The End of the Affair* Penguin Books, *The Heart of the Matter* Penguin Books, *The Power and the Glory* Penguin Books, *The Quiet American* Penguin Books.

ESSAYS AND SHORT STORIES

A Sense of Reality Penguin Books, *The Lost Childhood & Other Essays* Penguin Books, *Twenty-One Stories* W. Heinemann.*

PLAYS

The Living Room, The Potting Shed, The Complaisant Lover: all available in one volume:—Graham Greene *Three Plays* Mercury Paperbacks.

OTHER WORKS

A Sort of Life (Autobiographical) Bodley Head.*

FOR FURTHER READING

K. Allott & M. Farris: *The Art of Graham Greene* Hamish Hamilton,* David Pryce-Jones: in the Series *Writers and Critics* Oliver & Boyd.

D. H. LAWRENCE

NOVELS

Lady Chatterley's Lover Penguin Books or Four Square Paperbacks, *Sons and Lovers* Penguin Books, *The Plumed Serpent* Penguin Books, *The Rainbow* Penguin Books, *Women in Love* Penguin Books.

ESSAYS, SHORT STORIES, AND OTHER WORKS

England My England Penguin Books, *Love Among the Haystacks* Penguin Books, *Mornings in Mexico and Etruscan Places* Penguin Books, *Selected Essays* Penguin

SELECT BIBLIOGRAPHY

Books, *Selected Letters* Penguin Books, *Selected Poems* Penguin Books, *Twilight in Italy* Penguin Books.

FOR FURTHER READING
G. Hough: *The Dark Sun* Penguin Books, F. R. Leavis: *D. H. Lawrence: Novelist* Penguin Books.

KATHERINE MANSFIELD

SHORT STORIES
Bliss Penguin Books, *In a German Pension* Penguin Books, *Katherine Mansfield: Selected Stories* Oxford Paperbacks, *The Garden Party* Penguin Books.

FOR FURTHER READING
Katherine Mansfield and Other Literary Portraits Constable,* *The Letters of Katherine Mansfield* Constable.*

W. SOMERSET MAUGHAM

NOVELS
Cakes and Ale Penguin Books or Thorpe Paperbacks, *Of Human Bondage* Penguin Books, *The Moon and Sixpence* Penguin Books, *The Narrow Corner* Penguin Books, *The Painted Veil* Penguin Books, *The Razor's Edge* Penguin Books.

SHORT STORIES
Collected Short Stories Volumes 1–4 Penguin Books.

PLAYS
Selected Plays Penguin Books.

OTHER WORKS
The Summing Up (Autobiographical) Penguin Books.

FOR FURTHER READING
J. Brander: *Somerset Maugham* Oliver & Boyd,* J. Brophy: in the Series *Writers and Their Work* Longmans, R. Cordell: *Somerset Maugham* W. Heinemann,* R. Maugham: *Somerset and All the Maughams* W. Heinemann,* B. Nichols: *A Case of Human Bondage* Secker & Warburg,* Edited by G. Shivley: *Selected Prefaces and Introductions by Somerset Maugham* W. Heinemann.*

'SAKI' (H. H. MUNRO)

SHORT STORIES
Beasts and Superbeasts Macmillan Paperbacks, *The Best of 'SAKI'* (Edited by Graham Greene) Grey Arrow Paperbacks, *The Unbearable Bassington and Other Stories* Panther Paperbacks, *26 Short Stories* (Edited by E. V. Knox) Collins.*

FOR FURTHER READING
J. W. Lambert: Introduction to the *'Bodley Head SAKI'* Bodley Head.*

EVELYN WAUGH

NOVELS
A Handful of Dust Penguin Books, *Brideshead Revisited* Penguin Books, *Decline and Fall* Penguin Books, *Men at Arms* Penguin Books, *Officers and Gentlemen* Penguin Books, *Unconditional Surrender* Penguin Books, *Put Out More Flags* Penguin Books, *Scoop* Penguin Books, *The Loved One* Penguin Books, *Vile Bodies* Penguin Books.

SHORT STORIES AND TRAVEL BOOKS
The Ordeal of Gilbert Pinfold Penguin Books, *When the Going Was Good* Penguin Books.

FOR FURTHER READING
Frederick J. Stopp: *Evelyn Waugh: Portrait of an Artist* Chapman & Hall.*

VIRGINIA WOOLF

NOVELS
Between the Acts Hogarth Press,* *Jacob's Room* Penguin Books, *Mrs. Dalloway* Penguin Books, *Orlando* Penguin Books, *The Voyage Out* Hogarth Press,* *The Waves* Penguin Books, *To The Lighthouse* Penguin Books or Everyman Paperbacks.

ESSAYS, SHORT STORIES, AND OTHER WORKS
The Death of the Moth and Other Essays Penguin Books, *The Haunted House and Other Stories* Hogarth Press.*

FOR FURTHER READING
J. Bennett: *Virginia Woolf: Her Art as a Novelist* Cambridge University Press, E. M. Forster: *Virginia Woolf* Oliver & Boyd,* Quentin Bell: *Virginia Woolf: Volume One, Virginia Stephen 1882–1912: Volume Two, Mrs Woolf 1912–1941* Hogarth Press.*